'Practical, wise and very much based in reality, this book will make anyone running a business a more shrewd, and probably a more successful, leader.' Andrew Cahn, former CEO of UK Trade and Investment

'Cuts through turgid corporate "leadership speak" to get the heart of the matter – it should be required reading for any aspiring leader. If 'Fred the Shred' of HBOS had taken the Reality Test, perhaps we wouldn't be living through the biggest recession since the 1930s.' Lord Victor O. Adebowale CBE, CEO of Turning Point

'By approaching the perennial problems of business through a highly original set of emotionally-charged questions, Robert Rowland Smith brings an extraordinary array of insights to the challenges of management and leadership. Brilliant – a tour de force.' Jules Goddard, author of *Uncommon Sense, Common No*

**ROBERT ROWLAND SMITH** began his career as a Prize Fellow of All Souls College, Oxford. He went on to become a partner in a management consultancy. Today he works independently with the leaders of some of the world's foremost organisations, helping them tackle the realities of business. As well as writing several books, Robert has been a columnist for both the *Evening Standard* and *Sunday Times*. He is on the Faculty of the School of Life and the London Graduate School, and sits on the board of the Tavistock Institute of Medical Psychology. Robert also works with Oxford Business School on client engagements.

# THE REALITY TEST
## STILL RELYING ON STRATEGY?

**ROBERT ROWLAND SMITH**

PROFILE BOOKS

This paperback edition published in 2014

First published in Great Britain in 2013 by
PROFILE BOOKS LTD
3A Exmouth House
Pine Street
Exmouth Market
London EC1R 0JH
www.profilebooks.com

10 9 8 7 6 5 4 3 2 1

Typeset in Palatino by MacGuru Ltd
info@macguru.org.uk

Printed and bound in Great Britain by
CPI Group (UK) Ltd, Croydon CR0 4YY

A CIP catalogue record for this book is available from the British Library.

ISBN 978 1 78125 178 2
eISBN 978 1 84765 918 7

This book is based on my day-to-day experience over many years of advising a wide range of organisations, large and small, public and private, from different corners of the globe. I couldn't have had that experience without the clients who invited me in. I dedicate it to them.

*Few people have the imagination for reality.*
Goethe

# CONTENTS

*Preface*                                                          1

Part 1: **In the grand scheme of things**
*Introduction*                                                      7
1.  Who are you?                                                    9
2.  What's your organisation for?                                  14
3.  When will your business die?                                   18
4.  Will your organisation go to heaven?                           22
5.  Did the past never happen?                                     26
6.  Are you a vertical or a horizontal organisation?              30
7.  Are you sure you're adding any value?                          34
8.  Would you rather suffer than change?                           39
9.  Do you love money?                                             43
10. How much is enough?                                            47
11. What disasters are being born as you read this?               51
12. What are the unintended consequences?                          55

Part 2: **In the market**
*Introduction*                                                     61
13. Is your business an only child?                                63
14. Is your brand a mask or a window?                              68
15. What are your pheromones?                                      72
16. Would you buy what you sell?                                   76
17. Are your customers as real as you are?                         80

| | | |
|---|---|---|
| 18. | Is all your networking on expenses? | 84 |
| 19. | Is your business a sign of the times? | 88 |
| 20. | Are you making enough of your weaknesses? | 93 |
| 21. | Why aren't you predictable? | 98 |
| 22. | Are you searching for innovation where you expect to find it? | 101 |
| 23. | Do you want others to fail? | 105 |
| 24. | Do you even know what the market is? | 109 |

Part 3: **In your organisation**

| | | |
|---|---|---|
| *Introduction* | | 115 |
| 25. | Why isn't everything perfect? | 117 |
| 26. | Does your organisation face upwards, inwards or outwards? | 121 |
| 27. | What's the itch? | 125 |
| 28. | Is your organisation dumber than its people? | 129 |
| 29. | Do you have to play the game to fit in? | 132 |
| 30. | Is your business a happy family? | 136 |
| 31. | Which lies are acceptable? | 141 |
| 32. | What do you do with the spies? | 146 |
| 33. | How much dead wood should you carry? | 151 |
| 34. | Are you thinking too much about your culture? | 156 |
| 35. | How do you deal with the high-performing bad citizens? | 160 |
| 36. | Which card would cause the house to fall? | 165 |

Part 4: **In your head**

| | | |
|---|---|---|
| *Introduction* | | 171 |
| 37. | How much more valuable than your staff are you? | 173 |
| 38. | Whose love do you need? | 178 |
| 39. | Would you go down with your ship? | 182 |
| 40. | Shouldn't you be paranoid? | 187 |

41. When you shout, how high do they jump?                    191
42. Are you 100% productive 100% of the time?                 195
43. Are you lonely enough?                                    199
44. Does the autopilot need a rest?                           203
45. Are your decisions a science or an art?                   207
46. What do you tell yourself?                                212
47. What would you tell your therapist?                       216
48. What will they say when you've gone?                      220

*Epilogue*                                                    224
*Further Reading*                                             226
*Reader's Notes*                                              228
*Acknowledgements*                                            232
*Index*                                                       233

# PREFACE

'No strategy survives contact with the enemy.' It's a proverb I first heard while helping to run a discussion among the top brass of the Ministry of Defence, in London. Because it's based on estimates, a strategy is essentially a work of fiction. It can't stand up to the reality of war.

Business strategies are no less vulnerable than their military equivalents. Even strategies that are exemplars of analysis cannot account for all that will happen in the heat of business. Why? Because such strategies assume that business is as rational as themselves. Unfortunately, it's a lot messier than that. What gets in the way of the strategy's seamless execution is reality. That's what this book is about.

The obvious solution, you would think, is to load the strategy with as much reality as possible. But how?

You have to get beyond the typical strategy questions. Questions such as 'What is our revenue target?' or 'What is our market proposition?'. Being typical, they're easily replicated by the 'enemy', the competition. The result is that most strategies are variations on a small number of themes: grow, divest, diversify, consolidate, focus. And so the market fills up with companies pursuing very similar goals. Yet since some companies falter where others flourish, it's probably not those strategies that make the difference. They don't provide enough of a variable. Macroeconomic factors aside, the real reason businesses fail is that they run out of energy, or they don't believe in their product, or their leaders are too vain to heed advice, or they treat their customers like idiots, or they are sabotaged from within. Such are the realities that 'strategy' is too rational to account for.

The purpose of this book is to bring such realities into focus so that anyone leading a business will be equipped to deal with them. In order to make it easier for leaders to apply them to their own business I have explored these realities by answering a number of pointed questions. Three quick examples from the chapters ahead:

1. 'Did the past never happen?' I have seen too many organisations repeat mistakes because they don't take the time to learn lessons. Again, that's partly due to the obsession with strategy, which is all about the future; it's as if the past didn't exist. But because it actually happened, the past is more real than the future, which hasn't happened yet. It's a far more reliable source of information. I tell the story of a fashion house that keeps making the same errors because it only ever looks ahead.

2. 'Why isn't everything perfect?' Strategies often forget that organisations aren't perfectly honed delivery machines, but are made up of real people. I relate my experience of the organisation that tried to automate every possible process, only to realise that some decisions just couldn't be left to a machine. Only humans could compute the complex issues thrown up when what the strategy predicted fell foul of the reality that actually occurred.

3. 'What do you tell yourself?' As in real life, people in business sometimes believe things about themselves that

aren't true. In the case of one senior executive I coached, the gulf between his self-perception and the reality was vast. It was only as a result of being confronted with the reality that he could achieve the level of self-awareness necessary for him to change and for his colleagues to get behind him once more.

Real, pointed questions like these drive at the heart of what makes a business viable. They flush out the issues that most strategies do not. The issues can then be addressed and resolved. Conversely, if such questions aren't raised, the issues fester, and that can have disastrous consequences. Unasked is unarmed.

For example, I remember the law firm, now defunct, that every year vowed to shift from a model of 'premium services to premium clients for premium fees' to one of high-volume, low-margin transactional services for all and sundry. Their 'strategy' was to grow, and they didn't know how else to do this. Over the years, they edged towards the new model, but each time they edged a little further, one of the partners would leave. They might have wanted to grow, but they'd never posed the key question that growth implied: 'Do we want to change?' The answer would have been no – they liked their premium ways. Small wonder they died a slow death.

What I have done is pull together the most widely applicable of such questions from my experience of working as a consultant to boards and senior management teams (needless to say, I've disguised organisations and individuals to preserve confidentiality). The questions are designed to touch on the reality that strategy doesn't reach. As my background in philosophy taught me – in my twenties I was an Oxford don – asking one good question can shed more light than answering lots of bad ones.

Each question has a short chapter attached. The chapters can be read in any order, but I have grouped them to narrow in from the macro to the micro. The first group asks about how your business stands in the grand scheme of things; the last one probes what it's really like to be a leader. And although all of them suggest practical ways of changing your approach, they can be read simply as food for thought. Business is about doing, but the best doing is based on the best thinking.

# PART 1

# IN THE GRAND SCHEME OF THINGS

# INTRODUCTION

As its title suggests, this first part looks at your business in the widest possible perspective, the point being that businesses exist not only in the market but also in the real world. They are much more than players in a game of business strategy. They provide jobs for people, they make an impression on their customers, they pay tax to governments, they must satisfy their shareholders, they give to or take from society, and they are remembered or forgotten when they disappear.

One of the things that defines a business leader, as opposed to a manager, is that he or she is uniquely positioned to take in this broader perspective and hold it in mind. Not all leaders do so, of course: many become immersed in day-to-day management and forget that not all of business is about business.

It's not just the pressures of the day-to-day that impinge. The preoccupation in business with strategy means that the question of what the business is going to do leaves little room for questions of equal importance – not just *how* the business is going to deliver what the strategy demands, but *who* the business is, the character it has, the role it plays in the community, and so on.

So what kind of a business do you, as a leader, wish to be identified with? A successful one, for sure, but success is ultimately measured on more than making money – the widespread distaste for banks being a case in point. Why, after all, do people choose to go into different businesses? Because over and above making money, they hope to pursue a particular purpose: to build fine buildings, to find the cure for a disease, to provide amazing food, to push the boundaries of their profession, to develop themselves personally, to carry on a tradition, to make a difference. If strategy is about achieving commercial ambitions, then these other ambitions, which go beyond the commercial, need a lens other than strategy through which to view them.

# 1

# WHO ARE YOU?

One of my first assignments as a rookie consultant involved a high-street chemist, or drugstore. The funny thing was, you'd walk into a branch and not see any chemicals or drugs. Only if you zigzagged through the aisles to the back would you find a self-contained pharmacy. The pharmacy was stocked with arcane powders and staffed by apothecaries with faces as white as their coats, a breed apart from their made-up colleagues on the main floor. This floor featured everything from underwater cameras to umbrellas, sunglasses to sandwiches – even vibrators.

Custom was dwindling, and we naturally assumed it was because the offer in the stores was too confused. You couldn't tell if you were in an overgrown chemist or an under-grown supermarket. When we interviewed the high-ups about their market proposition, we met with an equally confused response. 'We're a pharmacy plus,' said one. 'We're a personal needs retailer,' said another. 'Feeling good or just feeling better – that's what we sell,' said an ingenious third.

The solution seemed obvious. They should slash the range of products and put the pharmacy at the centre. That would dispel the confusion in a trice, and customers would start flooding back. Yet as our interviews progressed, something else came to light. Despite the divergence of opinions, there was a common theme. It was to do with the company's history.

Having started as a small family business, the company won a place in the hearts of those who patronised it. Even though nationwide growth ensued, the company retained the provincial modesty that marked its beginnings. It managed to feel local in every location, and among its customers that translated into loyalty.

This insight steered us towards a sharper diagnosis. If once-loyal customers were now staying away, it wasn't because of the sprawl of products per se. After all, pure pharmacies themselves hold a dizzying array of stock – think of the pills, the phials, the potions, the unguents, the powders, the sprays, the drops, the capsules and the sachets. It was what the sprawl of non-pharmaceutical products implied. It implied the company just wanted to shift product, meaning that the relationship with the customer had become little more than transactional. Some of the spirit had gone.

The question we should have asked much sooner was not the one about market proposition, i.e. 'What's your core product?' That was too standard, too businessy, too 'strategic'. It led us to a generic answer about cutting back to the essentials. What we should have asked was: 'Who are you?' Had we asked that, we would have got to something more real more quickly. The answer would have been along the lines of 'We are the people who provide local and trustworthy expertise about your health. That expertise manifests itself as both advice from your pharmacist and a carefully chosen selection of products that we recommend for your general well-being.'

This answer tempered the initial instinct to lop off every limb of the business which wasn't the pharmacy. At the same time, it put limits on what kind of non-pharmaceutical products could be sold: suntan lotion, yes, because it protects against skin cancer; cameras and crisps, probably not. It was as if the store were an extension of the GP on the high street, a benevolent presence to whom customers would feel ready to give their loyalty once more.

In this case, the question 'Who are you?' uncovered the identity of the business and the extent to which customers had subconsciously become invested in it. Messing with that identity by offering too many non-pharmaceutical, and specifically non-health-related, products was creating among customers something more serious than confusion. They felt disappointed, even betrayed. Bringing that identity back into view helped to restore faith.

Is the moral of the story that businesses should stick to their knitting? Were it so, it would put the kibosh on any innovation or diversification. Thankfully, it is not. The company would be able to sell a range of non-pharmaceutical products, just as long as they fitted inside the framework of the 'GP on the high street'. This framework didn't preclude growth or creativity, it just provided the guide-rails to grow or create within. Understanding who you are helps to identify that framework.

The moral therefore is 'be yourself'. This is different from just doing what you've always done, because it does allow for growth. Most importantly, it's about realising what's unique about your business.

Too many businesses struggle to answer the question of who they are, because they can't articulate what's unique. Go, for example, to the website of pretty much any professional services firm – lawyers, accountants, financial advisers – and you'll find they are mere variations on the theme of 'providing solutions to client issues'. On the surface, many such businesses exist simply because there's a general demand for professional services from customers and a general need for employment from graduates. But knowing who you are and then projecting it to customers can bring enormous business benefit. It can make you stand out and so attract those customers to you.

By the same token, not knowing who you are can have disastrous consequences. Take the unhappy tale of Cisco and Flip. It's 2007. The figure cut by Cisco is that of a technology giant, focused on the business-to-business market, and known for serious heft in developing enterprise networking systems. Flip, by contrast, is a funky start-up that in true Silicon Valley style has been kicked off by a band of entrepreneurs in an office above Gump's department store in San Francisco. Their particular gizmo is the Flip video camera. It's lightweight, inexpensive, easy to use and cool. Making traditional 'camcorders' look like bricks, it becomes an instant hit. In its first two years it ships two million units.

In 2009 Cisco bought Flip for $590m, suggesting a new strategic intent to reach into the consumer market. Like so many strategies, however, this strategy had a blind spot in the form of reality. It wasn't the price of the acquisition, eye-watering though that was. Nor was it that the acquisition wasn't attractive: if you had that kind of money to invest, why wouldn't you invest in such a promising prospect? However, the reality was that the firms were chalk and cheese. By April 2011, barely two years later, Cisco had shut its new division down. Yes, there were contributory factors, especially the improved video on smartphones, but these were only part of the story. The *New York Times* ran the following quote:

> 'Cisco was swayed by the sexiness of selling to the consumer,' said Mo Koyfman, a principal at Spark Capital, a Boston venture capital firm. 'They're not wired to do it themselves, so they do it by acquisition. Flip was one of the most visible tar-

gets out there. But it's really hard to turn an elephant into a horse. Cisco's an elephant.'

At a fundamental level, Cisco existed to be Cisco, and Flip existed to be Flip. Like trying to cross a horse with an elephant, combining Cisco's and Flip's DNA just didn't work. The moral therefore is that it's not what you're selling, it's who you are. From that, everything else follows.

# 2

# WHAT'S YOUR ORGANISATION FOR?

Perhaps the best answer to the question 'What is your organisation for?' is: 'To deliver my enterprise's purpose'. And yet, in my experience, organisations aren't always organised with that fundamental purpose in mind. Instead they are organised according to what's most convenient for the senior managers; or they're organised in the way that someone had organised them previously; or they're organised around where the company happens to have offices. And cynics will argue that in the public sector, organisations are organised to provide a workplace for those who might otherwise be unemployed. In terms of the purpose of the enterprise, their activity will be nugatory, but it keeps them off the streets, saves welfare spend, and helps their self-esteem.

It's a good test to consider how you would deliver your fundamental purpose if you had no organisation at all. Taking things down to zero in this way forces you to think hard about what organisational resources you actually need. Let's take an absurd example. Say your purpose was to put Samsung out of business. It doesn't follow that you have to compete with them. You could, in theory, raise the necessary capital, buy Samsung and close it down. No 'organisation' required.

Or take a less extreme example. Here's the mission statement from Starbucks:

Our mission: to inspire and nurture the human spirit – one person, one cup and one neighborhood at a time

What kind of organisation does that require? It's not obvious that serving coffee is the best route to inspiring and nurturing the human spirit. If that is your purpose, you might be better off modelling yourself on the Dalai Lama rather than setting up an international beverage retailer with a reputation for avoiding taxes. But if you restrict yourself to inspiring and nurturing the human spirit through coffee 'one person, one cup and one neighborhood at a time', you're in a different game. Now you need to figure out how to put a cup of coffee into the hands of what sounds like every single person on the planet. That certainly requires some organising. It probably requires an organisation.

Although I'm being somewhat tongue-in-cheek, the Starbucks example does help us understand what organisations are for. Like distributing food aid to refugees, getting coffee out to such a vast population of consumers calls for fairly weighty operational resources. This operational perspective reminds us that the primary purpose of an organisation (as opposed to an enterprise) is to organise the work rather than the people. In other words, you should organise the process before you organise the structure – form following function, of course.

Is that it? Not quite. Think of soccer teams, and how they are organised. Their purpose is to win matches. From this purpose you might infer that they should organise themselves to score goals, which would mean having eleven centre forwards. But that would leave them vulnerable at the back, and they'd have to score more and more goals to compensate for all the goals they were conceding to the opposition. An essential part of winning, in other words, is not losing. So soccer teams organise themselves both to win and to not lose. Midfielders adapt to where the balance of offence and defence lies at any given moment.

In business, analogies with sport are two a penny, of course, but this concept of organising your company not just to win but not to lose has some mileage in it. Business leaders and business books bang on about 'winning' and 'winning strategies', but winning isn't achieved by creating a one-dimensional team of forwards. The reality is that you must have a defence too. How do you protect yourself against the opposition? How do you organise yourselves so that you're not just following your own purpose but thwarting the purpose of another enterprise that's organised itself to exploit your weaknesses?

The answer lies in getting the basics right. Boring, perhaps, but so important. Just as you organise your forwards to be innovative and ambitious, you've got to organise your defenders to cover the business essentials. The biggest economic crisis in the Western world for decades was created because banks were lending to people who couldn't afford to repay them. Mistakes don't come much more basic than that. These banks were well organised for attack – that's what the assault on the sub-prime market was all about – but were poorly organised for defence. In those banking organisations, the balance between the investor types and the risk management types had got out of whack. They were organised to win, no doubt about it, but they were not organised not to lose, which is the other half of the equation.

So go ahead and organise your organisation around your purpose, a purpose which will be a positive, goal-scoring purpose. Absolutely. But don't forget to cover the basics at the other end. And remember that the main way of not winning is losing.

# 3

# WHEN WILL YOUR BUSINESS DIE?

*Built to Last* by Jim Collins and Jerry I. Porras is a remarkable book. It describes the ingredients that go into making a long-lasting company, and looks set to make old bones of its own. First published in 1994, it has become that rare item among the many business books produced each year: a classic. And what this classic book reveals about the classic companies that fall under its microscope is that they last a long time thanks less to the staples of management practice, such as cost reduction or quality control, than to their 'visionary' qualities. Along with the 'big hairy audacious goals' coined by the authors, these qualities include the values such companies espouse.

That is the explicit point the authors wish to make, but there's an implicit point too. Namely, that longevity in business is mighty hard to achieve. Those long-lasting companies are very much the exception; the norm is nearer ten years. Many companies will start up with a dream of outlasting the field, but the dream becomes real for all too few.

And yet longevity is only longevity; by no means is the word interchangeable with 'success', despite what the *Built to Last* project might lead us to think. You can be successful and short-lived, especially if you sell at that ten-year point to a generous buyer. Indeed, given that the chances of your own business joining the ranks of Collins and Porras's visionary companies are discouragingly low, actively planning its end may be the wiser course. Being realistic on this score liberates you to focus on a shorter time horizon, a horizon more in your control. As with any plan, it's better to start with the end and work backwards, than set off with no clear sense of the final destination. Imagine the reverse. Imagine being in a firm that limps along for years like a wounded fox, rather than being put out of its misery. The reality is that lasting isn't always noble.

Especially if you are a tobacco company. In the year 2000, I had a meeting with British American Tobacco (BAT), at their headquarters on the Strand in London. I still remember my surprise at walking into an office of such corporate style and swagger to find it reeking of smoke. In the reception area, complimentary cigarettes were put out for visitors, and in the meeting itself several BAT staff would – with neither permission nor shame – light up. I also remember the unease I felt: shouldn't consultants draw the line somewhere in terms of whose shilling they are prepared to accept?

As it happens, my involvement with BAT lasted no more than a few hours, so the question faded away, and my conscience was never properly tested. But what remained was the sheer fact that the company continued to be successful, despite mounting pressure on the industry; it was on the verge of celebrating its first centenary, no less. Founded in 1902, British American Tobacco – unlike many of its consumers – seemed in fine fettle. And so it has continued to this day, despite the threat of stringent new laws forbidding branding even on cigarette packs themselves.

When BAT will die is therefore a moot point. For it has indeed survived, and may even continue for some time longer, the reality being that while more educated parts of the world have largely kicked the nicotine habit, other places are yet to hear, let alone heed, the message about the dangers of smoking. So the lack of education can be exploited. Or, to phrase it from the producers' point of view, there is still room for market penetration.

But it's a race against time. Sooner or later the public health message will have reached all four corners of the globe, and BAT will be a busted flush. It's not a question of whether it will die, but when. Is it better therefore for BAT to take matters into its own hands, and set a suicide date to work back from? Apart from anything else, it would be sparing itself from more lawsuits, more public vilification.

In short, the art of 'knowing when to go' can be applied as much to companies as individuals, for whom carrying on for too long becomes unseemly. In both cases, reality gets covered up by vague optimism or vain denial. We all know that the days of BAT are numbered, so a staged wind-down might be more fitting. The difference, of course, is that individuals are organic beings, whose death is built in, which means in terms of career, they know there's an unavoidable decline to manage. Companies may employ organic beings, but are capable of surviving them. They are economic entities, and economic entities have no predetermined lifespan. This encourages the people running them to believe their companies are potentially immortal.

That said, a dip into Wikipedia's roster of oldest companies will tell you that one or two have come close. Japan's Kongo Gumi, a construction company, existed from the jaw-droppingly early date of 578 until 2006. That's 1,428 years. How did it attain such old age? As an article in *Business Week* put it: 'Kongo Gumi's case suggests that it's a good idea to operate in a stable industry. Few industries could be less flighty than Buddhist temple construction.'

So Kongo Gumi was in the temple-building business, a business that, compared to tobacco, might seem impregnable. But as the same article goes on to point out, it suffered from equally modern woes:

> The circumstances of Kongo Gumi's demise also offer some lessons. Despite its incredible history, it was a set of ordinary circumstances that brought Kongo Gumi down at last. Two factors were primarily responsible. First, during the 1980s bubble economy in Japan, the company borrowed heavily to invest in real estate. After the bubble burst in the 1992–93 recession, the assets secured by Kongo Gumi's debt shrank in value. Second, social changes in Japan brought about declining contributions to temples. As a result, demand for Kongo Gumi's temple-building services dropped sharply beginning in 1998.

So, when will your business die? What the stories of BAT and Kongo Gumi tell us is that context is key – not just 'strategic context' but paradigm shifts and alterations in the zeitgeist. If medical research discovers that cigarettes are bad for you, where previously they were considered beneficial; or if growing secularisation means you can't garner enough support to keep your temple going; then these are factors you couldn't have predicted at the outset, and that lie beyond your control. C'est la vie. But once you know the factors are there, that the context is changing for the worse, it's better to get out while the going's good.

**4**

# WILL YOUR ORGANISATION GO TO HEAVEN?

I write this from a hotel room in the Roppongi district of central Tokyo. I'm here for a busy week of meetings with senior executives from some of Japan's most iconic companies, including the likes of Hitachi and Mitsubishi. Earlier today I attended a 'CEO Growth Congress' hosted by the *Economist*. The word 'growth' is key because – at least until the arrival of 'Abenomics' – it's the thing that Japan has been finding so elusive. As to why that is the case, the consensus view goes something like the following.

The Second World War was a watershed in Japanese history. Hiroshima destroyed so much, not just in terms of loss of life, but in terms of the national psyche, that the only response was to start again from scratch. What emerged were some of those famous companies – Sony is another example – even if other major brands such as Toyota, Olympus and Fujitsu were already up and running some time before. The post-war effort led to a golden era of Japanese business that lasted more or less unbroken until the Asian financial crisis of the 1990s. Since then, exacerbated by the West's own financial crisis of the noughties plus the tsunami of '3/11', the country and its corporates have been in the doldrums. Returning to the growth path is hampered not only by global conditions such as European sovereign debt and slowing growth in China, but by internal factors. Among these are an ageing population and the fact that those large corporates are tired, old-fashioned and inward-looking.

I use the word 'corporates' as if such organisations were exclusively commercial entities. But the fact that their fate has been so linked with that of the country as a whole means that they do not exist in a cordoned-off commercial sphere. They are closer in profile to national institutions, even if technically they're not owned or operated by the state. I'd argue that they are a hybrid of the commercial and the national, so long as by 'national' we understand something that is not 'national-ised' but that holds deep symbolism for the Japanese nation as a whole. They were, and to some extent still are, part of the national effort, not just a cluster of weighty private enterprises.

The point is that among the Japanese there appears to be an assumed sense of identity with such organisations, and that this is very different from the West, where companies have to prove their social worth. Even if some of those seminal names in Japanese business do bite the dust – and it's hard to believe that they can all survive – they will be assured of their place in heaven. They will have done good things for the collective effort, and despite their inability to modernise will continue to be thought of well, long after their demise.

Although Western companies want to be thought well of too, most start from a place that lies a considerable distance from the national effort or the needs of society. As if to compen-sate somewhat, their conscience moves them to engage in 'corporate social responsibility', sponsoring community projects, donating to charity, supporting local schools. It's not completely disinterested, however, because the tacit hope is that such efforts will reflect well on the brand. In the final analysis, company always comes before country. Generally speaking, the Western corporation will not tie its agenda to that of the nation in which it is headquartered. In addition, the globalisation of businesses drives a wedge between company and nation, because becoming global means becoming supranational, floating above national concerns and operating instead in an international economy that has little time for national imperatives – except insofar as these impose tax rules, governance frameworks or export controls.

The net result is that it remains difficult for Western companies to feel they deserve a place in heaven. They've made a pact with a commercial world that's largely separate from the interests of the nation or the society. You could probably mount an argument that capitalism itself is defined by not being constrained by such interests. Or at least you could argue the reverse, i.e. that capitalism's antagonists, socialism and communism, certainly are tied into the nation and its social priorities.

So what can the Western business leader do? Ironically enough, an answer might yet be found on the islands of Japan. Take Rakuten, the Japanese Internet retailer that has its sights set on unseating Amazon, no less. Currently Rakuten is on the acquisition trail, buying up Internet retailers around the globe, and driving towards the goal advertised so nakedly on its website: to be the world's leading virtual mall. Rakuten's differentiator as explained to me this week, however, is that it really cares about both its vendors and its customers. It sees itself as setting up a market in which traders can trade and make a decent living. It sees itself as offering consumers the chance to improve their quality of life, not just shop for stuff. Indeed, its founder and leader, Hiroshi Mikitani, has published a book stressing the importance of the good society.

Although the Rakuten project could hardly differ more on the surface from the post-war reconstruction of Japan, there are some carry-overs. Whether it has a viable economic formula or not, Rakuten's aim to include the prosperity of both vendors and customers in its own plans reflects that perhaps uniquely Japanese ability to think both commerce and country at the same time. Whether Rakuten will go to heaven or not, I do not know, but the model is an interesting one.

There are other possibilities too for the Western company that wishes to pass through the pearly gates. Even Amazon, which seems so unalloyed an example of supra-national self-interest, has redeeming features. It pioneered the very clicks-and-mortar environment that Rakuten now gleefully exploits, which made it feasible for small traders, previously debarred from the high street by prohibitive rents, to compete against the big guns; a model that could be described as commercial democracy in action. It also allows authors to self-publish, thus reducing the costs incurred in working through an agent; again one can read this as democracy, if not quite as nation-building. Of course, there are plenty of other ways in which it crushes those around it, but in this limited sense it creates a bottom-up version of good society, as opposed to the more top-down Japanese model. Not to mention the mutual, the increasingly fashionable operating form in which employees take a share of the business and/or the profits. Again, it's a model that stops short of 'nation-building' in the Japanese sense, but at least it moderates the notion of profit as the cream taken from the top by a few fat cats who are domiciled not in their home country but wherever the tax regime is most clement.

Naturally, 'heaven' is only a metaphor for the social worth of your enterprise. But like it or not, your enterprise will indeed have a social worth, apart from any commercial value. All things considered, it's better for that worth to be high rather than low.

# 5

# DID THE PAST NEVER HAPPEN?

I am sitting with Steven and Wendy, CEO and COO respectively of a fashion house. In order to have as free and frank a discussion as possible, we have agreed to meet away from the office, in Wendy's home, an elegant brownstone on the Lower East Side. They are using this confidential setting to moan at great length about the company's finance director; let's call him John.

The trouble with John, they say, is that he feels no responsibility for the business. Yes, he does his job, but he never arrives early or leaves late, and no one has ever seen him break a sweat. What John wants, they say, is to go on drawing his substantial salary and make sure he's home in time for dinner in Westchester with his wife, his family and their dogs. This doesn't stop him hitting on his secretary, by the way, which is merely another sign of him just doing whatever makes him feel good and hanging the consequences. Regarding the company as a whole, he appears to have no sense of ownership, or realisation that the money he makes has to be earned every day by those who are going the extra mile.

The obvious solution to the John question was to sack him. But that would have been to treat a symptom rather than dealing with the underlying cause. Before Steven and Wendy began their whingeing, they had been telling me the history of the firm. Steven was the founder along with an original finance director called Nathan. Steven never respected Nathan, mainly because Nathan never seemed to be shouldering his share of the burden, leaving Steven to do more of the work. Before long, Nathan left, never to be heard from again. Nathan's replacement was Carlos. Guess what? Steven never respected Carlos, mainly because Carlos never seemed to be shouldering his share of the burden, leaving Steven to do more of the work. When Carlos left, he was replaced by John. The pattern was even more obvious than the supposedly obvious solution.

The real issue with John was that he had been framed by Steven. He had been put in a mental frame that was originally created for Nathan. Steven looked into this frame with contempt. It allowed Steven to feel superior, to feel good about the outstanding level of his own contribution to the company he co-founded. But it was a feeling he could generate only by positioning someone else as correspondingly inferior. Secretly, Steven loved John's lack of responsibility. It was this love that gave him the energy to moan for so long about him. It was the expression less of a pressing business challenge, and more of a psychological issue from much earlier.

In general, organisations are preoccupied with the present and the future, and pay scant regard to the past. That's hardly surprising: the present is right here, right now, demanding attention. The fixation in the business world with strategy means there's a sometimes frenzied emphasis on 'getting to the future first'. Just look at how often the word 'tomorrow' features in business advertisements, for example. But there is a cost to this imbalance, a cost neatly exemplified by our New York fashion house. Not dealing with the past makes it more likely to return. What's more, it can return in ways you're not even aware of unless you take a step back and look at your history.

There is another lesson, not from psychology but from chaos theory. It speaks of the law of 'sensitive dependence on initial conditions'. What happens in the early moments of any phenomenon has an effect on its future that is disproportionately larger than the effect produced by events that come later. The Big Bang would be a good example, because what took place in the first trillionth of a second decisively shaped the future of the universe. When Steven and Nathan first got together to form their company, there was already a flaw. The founders weren't quite in it to the same degree. Or at least Steven was ready to see Nathan as less in it than he was; so ready, perhaps, that Nathan ended up acting out Steven's idea about him, like a self-fulfilling prophecy. This initial set-up of the firm and the original asymmetry between the two founders that was built into it was destined to influence later events.

Actually, we don't need either psychology or chaos theory to appreciate such truths. Anyone who has started a business will have had a sense of the quality of its founding. Was there a good feeling? Was there a good spirit? Or was it set up awry, with miscommunication among those involved, unclear expectations, or a poorly conceived purpose? The founding moment lasts into the present and into the future. It's worth getting it right, and it's worth stopping early if you know something is wrong.

A quick footnote: a few days ago I walked past a restaurant opening up in my neighbourhood. The new owners – two women in their thirties – were sitting at one of the outside tables, going through figures, while painters were refurbishing the interior. It will be a Thai place. On the same site, before it, there was a pizza joint that lasted about a year. Before that, an African eatery that only managed six months. Before that, a brasserie for a year. And before the brasserie, when we moved into the area, it was a 'modern European' restaurant. Clearly, another repeating pattern, this time to do with the location itself – for locations have histories as much as businesses do. There's little those new owners can do to lay whatever ghosts still hover from the first business – in every sense, it's not their concern. But I nearly stopped to tell them they should spend a moment or two respecting what had gone before them on that site and asking for some sort of blessing. Not to mention making sure they are fully in it together.

# 6

# ARE YOU A VERTICAL OR A HORIZONTAL ORGANISATION?

Andrew Solomon's book *Far from the Tree* talks about the difference between 'vertical' and 'horizontal' identity. The difference depends on how closely you follow your parents – how 'far from the tree' of your parents you, the apple, have fallen. For example, if you are a car mechanic called John Smith Junior and you work for a garage called John Smith Senior and Sons, your identity is vertical. If your mother was a hippy and you are the female chief executive of a large manufacturing operation, you are horizontal.

Of course, there will be people who fall between the horizontal and vertical stools, and some who are both, but the distinction makes for a handy framework for understanding identity, or at least a good way of structuring a debate. I think it can be adapted to organisations. A vertical organisation is based on command-and-control, whereby orders issued at the top are obediently followed by those down the line. The classic example would be the army. A horizontal organisation, by contrast, works far more on consensus. Think perhaps of a research laboratory where data has to be pooled from among many scientists, and there's no one right way of doing things.

As the examples of the army and the research lab imply, it's not necessarily better to be either vertical or horizontal. The one isn't superior to the other. What matters is that the organisation chooses the model most conducive to the kind of work it does. If the outcome you seek is to win a firefight on the streets of Beirut, it's probably best if the soldiers concerned follow the orders they are given, rather than going it alone. Alternatively, if your desired outcome is a cure for cancer, you may well make more progress by challenging assumptions and even questioning the basis of the research itself.

Unfortunately, many businesses believe they are horizontal when the reality is that they are vertical. But the reality has to come first, whatever one's strategic aspirations. Even the research lab suffers a bit from this delusion. Think of the disgruntlement expressed by many academics towards 'management'; their heartfelt belief is that theirs is a horizontal world of intellectual exploration rather than obedience, and they resent the reframing of the academy as a vertical entity in which they perceive themselves as becoming mere units of production in a corporate effort they don't endorse. There is some ideological context to this phenomenon. In the West in particular, democracy is highly prized, so Western organisations are predisposed to 'democratic' practices in the workplace, i.e. operating on a consensus model, which is considered inclusive, rather than command-and-control, which is seen as anti-democratic or authoritarian.

I will give an example from the world of TV and film production. Having been involved in various projects, mainly as a 'talking head' for TV shows though once or twice as an actor, I have witnessed a range of approaches. At one end of the spectrum, I have taken part in shoots that have gone on and on for hours as the cameraman debates the merits of different lighting effects, the sound engineer plays with his levels, the costume designer argues for a different look, and there are numerous time-outs in which the whole crew weighs up the alternatives. It's a creative industry and the presumption is that someone might just come up with something brilliant at any moment. But as the huddle is being had, the light is fading, everyone's getting hungry, personal arrangements are having to be reshuffled and the energy starts to wilt.

This horizontal approach doesn't work because the truth is that, despite the 'creative' context, TV and film production is a highly vertical business; this is a parallel to adopting a strategy that lies at odds with reality. Many elements – light, sound, image, voice – have to be brought together into a tight, coherent whole for the viewer. So many elements, in fact, that the permutations are probably infinite. Given that range of possibilities, there has to be some arbitration. Someone has to make an 'arbitrary' decision, in the best sense; not arbitrary meaning 'random' or 'thoughtless', but arbitrary meaning taking responsibility for a decision in the face of limitless choices and the risk of no decision being taken at all.

And so, at the other end of the spectrum, I have just come off the set of a short film where I saw such arbitrary decisions being made, and the result was much more satisfying for all concerned. I am referring to the directness of the director. She was able to corral a whole team of young people in jeans and trainers, and focus them on the task at hand. This didn't mean she ignored what they had to say – she wasn't notably 'authoritarian' – but it was clear that she was wholly focused on the outcome. Her decision-making had a professional briskness that kept the energy on set at a fine point. She saw that despite appearances she was in a vertical world, and she chose the vertical approach.

The best example I can give of a horizontal approach in a horizontal world is that of the think tank, which has the freedom I mentioned as being so prized by academics, but less of the managerial infrastructure. As the name suggests, the core purpose of a think tank is to think. Although the thinking might eventuate in real things like articles and policy documents, the value lies in the richness of the process that's gone into producing them. This richness requires a mixture of viewpoints. The think tanks of which I have seen the inner workings put a premium, therefore, on diversity of thought within their organisations, as well as on consulting outsiders, people from other walks of life whose experiences run against the norm. These organisations tend to be very flat in structure, and the people who lead them don't really 'lead' much at all; they act as much as facilitators of debate as setters of tasks, hubs around which conversation revolves. A different leadership style, with edicts issued from the top, would serve only to cut off such conversation in its prime.

The lesson for business leaders is to define the outcome your business is seeking to achieve, and adapt the management style accordingly.

# 7

# ARE YOU SURE YOU'RE
# ADDING ANY VALUE?

Some time ago a client made a comment that nettled me. She was musing about the off-site I was to facilitate for her and her top leadership cadre of about thirty people, who were normally dispersed across different locations. As we discussed the design for the two-day event, we agreed we must allow time on the agenda for people to network. After all, in feedback after such events it's nearly always 'the opportunity to spend time with colleagues' that heads the list of things that delegates appreciated most. So quite pertinently my client asked, 'Is there any value you can add that's greater than bringing people together in a room and letting them get on with it?'

Fair cop, I thought. Although a bit of me wanted to justify my large fee by coming up with a fancy agenda, another bit of me knew she was right. Over many years of facilitating top team meetings, I've come in any case to understand that an agenda, or a workshop design, is a ladder to be thrown away. You have to have an agenda, otherwise people won't take the event seriously or will fret about whether it's the best use of their time. But you have to be prepared to abandon it, or the conversation that takes place among the leaders becomes a slave to the agenda, whereas it should be the other way round: the agenda must serve the conversation, and get out of the way when it doesn't. These days, with the clients I've supported the longest, those who know and trust me the most, we'll barely set an agenda at all. The event will be billed simply as 'Board Retreat' or 'Top Team Off-Site', facilitated by yours truly. The one thing we might decide in advance is the most important question that the company needs to ask and that only the senior people gathered can answer. With that question in our cross-hairs, the session generally goes well. Sometimes a substantial portion of the session itself is dedicated to articulating the question, on the grounds that (a) asking the right question gets you more than halfway to finding the right answer, and (b) the process of uncovering it affords a great deal of insight.

My client's piercing comment also set me thinking about the very definition of value. Heaven knows we talk enough about it. I believe there are two helpful answers to the question, one classic, one contemporary.

The classic answer comes from a consumer or retail perspective. Value resides in the space, the 'delta' as it's known, between price and quality. It is not simply a question of how cheap something is: quality is the other axis. The lower the price and the higher the quality of the product I purchase, the greater the value, and vice versa. The buyer makes a free judgement accordingly, especially in a capitalist or free-market system which gives him or her the liberty of comparing value among several products. In this sphere of relative judgements, there is, however, an absolute limit for the customer in going for the best value product. This absolute limit is affordability. A Prada handbag, for example, might actually be better value than a Primark handbag, but for most people the price puts it out of reach. Value operates within bands of affordability.

The seller, meanwhile, has to keep an eye not only on the competition but on cost, which is the seller's equivalent of the buyer's affordability. The instinct will be to maintain price and to reduce quality, because for the seller the delta is margin. Hence another equivalent: margin is to the seller what value is to the buyer. Against this instinct for margin, the seller has the option of trusting in the promise of market share. That is, over time buyers should realise where the best value to be had lies, and keep coming back; they will likely attract other buyers into the bargain. If as a seller you keep your nerve by offering the best value, the chances are you will rise in the market.

So much for the classic answer as to what value is. Elemental it may be, but because it's based on a market for products, it only goes so far. The truth is that capitalist markets trade in things far more intangible than products, things like services, whose value is harder to measure. In fact, the drift towards intangibility appears to define late capitalism, and I think it goes much further than services, into brand and even 'meaning', which promises the greatest value of all. And what do I mean by 'meaning'? I mean ideas that consumers can apply to their own life.

I can illustrate my theory through an analogy with Abraham Maslow's famous hierarchy of human needs. Broadly speaking, Maslow argues that humans have an instinct for higher things, the things that make it worthwhile being a human being. As against animals, only human beings have the ability for such rarefied states as 'self-actualisation', which is the ultimate realisation of human potential. In this state, we know who we are, have begun executing our fundamental purpose in the world, and achieve an almost spiritual contentment. Unfortunately, we can't get to this elevated plane before some basics have been fulfilled. There's little point trying to self-actualise if you're starving and don't have a roof over your head. Only once such necessities are satisfied can we go on to create relationships with each other, to build a good society, and eventually, perhaps, to self-actualise, the ultimate value.

It's this upwards movement towards the intangible that we see in capitalism, as it moves along the value scale from products to services to brand to meaning. Most of us are fortunate enough to have our basic needs met, and rightly or wrongly we're on the lookout for more. Take the example of owning a car. In the early days of car manufacturing, I am simply pleased to own a car that gets me from A to B. Before long, however, I want some services to go with my car. I want to get it washed, for example. So I take the product, the car, for granted, and begin to look for add-ons to make me feel better about it. Next, I notice my car isn't as cool as my neighbour's car. New cars have come on to the market. They all go from A to B, and they can all be kept clean, but some stand out, and seem more valuable, even though they're not necessarily more expensive. I want the cooler brand.

Or at least I did. We late capitalist consumers are familiar to the point of boredom with products, services and even brands. The value we can extract from them seems pretty finite. We always want more, and the next and perhaps final step in terms of capitalist value will almost certainly lie in what I'm calling meaning. So now I want to know what it means for me to drive at all: what kind of a person am I if I drive? Am I spoiling the planet? Can Land Rover or Volkswagen or Pontiac fill the paradoxical hole that consumption leaves in me? Can they tell me something interesting? Can they offer me ways to improve my life? Can they connect me to an idea I haven't thought of?

Don't get me wrong. Products will still need to prove their value in that delta between price and quality. But that's just the bottom end of the market. The upper end is where the growth lies, and where a whole continent of value remains to be mined. My reason for saying this is that the driver (no pun) of capitalist consumption is the pleasure that that consumer experiences. Owning products gives me some pleasure, using services gives me pleasure, and basking in a brand gives me pleasure too. But there's nothing quite so pleasurable to consume as a great idea that really speaks to me – what I'm calling 'meaning'.

It's a logic that again highlights the limits of classic business strategy, which tends to occupy itself with products and services. True, many companies will have a brand strategy too, but very few indeed will be thinking how they can add meaning to the lives of their customers. Those who do will win the day.

# 8

# WOULD YOU RATHER SUFFER THAN CHANGE?

Kennedy's Sausages was a family-run business based in London. Founded in 1877, it started running into trouble in the 1990s. Custom was dwindling. Strange, because during the same period there was something of a boom in the sausage market. Where once sausages had been seen as an unglamorous basic, a staple for a school dinner or a functional supper, they were becoming fashionable, albeit in a somewhat ironic way. Gourmet sausages with higher meat content, less rusk, and flavours ranging from pork and apple to lamb and mint, were finding their way not just into high-end butcher's shops but also supermarkets; Toulouse sausage with parsley mash and red onion gravy was a dish you might serve up at a dinner party. Bangers were booming.

But as they boomed, Kennedy's began to bust. The company cited competition from those supermarkets, but that wasn't the whole story. They failed to respond. They continued to sell the sausages they'd always sold. The fact that they neglected the physical appearance of their shops didn't help. To the casual observer it seemed they simply couldn't keep up with the times. But stranger still was the fact that they knew it. It is said that the staff would plead with the owner to modernise the business and capitalise on the new demand. It is said that he stubbornly refused. The consequence was that in 2007 Kennedy's went out of business. To this day, there are one or two vacant Kennedy's premises, with the old-fashioned lettering of the shop name coming away like teeth.

It's a sad story, but it contains a valuable lesson for anyone running a business. Namely, the instinct to carry on doing the same thing is often stronger than the instinct to change, even when doing the same thing is causing you to suffer. Even when you know what you need to do to fix things. Even when there is a market ready to beat down your door if only you make the changes so glaring to everyone else. As paradoxical as it sounds, we would sometimes rather suffer than change.

In the case of Kennedy's, the thing that needed changing was more fundamental than the type of sausages they sold or the lighting in their shops. It was the attitude of the owners. A business is an expression of the psychology of the most powerful people in it. From its aggressiveness in the market you can infer the mindset of the top dogs at, say, JPMorgan Chase, just as from its campaigns you know the beliefs of the head honchos at Oxfam. It is in such attitudes, psychologies, mindsets and beliefs that the destiny of a business resides. And they are hard to get at precisely because they lodge inside people's heads; like the engine under the bonnet of a car, they can't be worked on from outside.

Hence the rise of change management, the theory and practice of causing shifts in organisational culture ('Shift Happens', to quote the droll name of a client's change initiative). Whether or not businesses are wedded to their suffering, their default will be to do more of the same rather than anything different. The reason, according to the formula developed by Richard Beckhard, is that what's different tends not to be compelling enough to stimulate such a shift.

According to the formula, change can occur only when the perceived cost of change (not just in money terms) is less than the combined power of the following: dissatisfaction with the present, a vision of the future, and some clear first steps towards it that can be taken.

In my experience, it is the first of these three – dissatisfaction with the present – that is at once the most decisive and the least addressed. Organisations who conclude that a change needs to be made will readily debate their vision and just as readily agree some next steps in the form of actions that can be taken away. That is the bread and butter of change management, but it's not the meat in the sandwich, pork or otherwise. Without genuine dissatisfaction, without real and present pain, that visioning is for the birds. As in the argument of *Who Moved My Cheese?*, the problem is partly that people find it harder to credit the dire consequences of not changing than to pin their hopes on what's before their eyes. So the future pain has to be made real and personal. It's not enough to announce to people, 'This business is going under.' You have to say, 'You're going to lose your job.' Beckhard's 'dissatisfaction with the present' has to be visceral. I would strengthen his rather mild phrasing to read something like 'individual fear of imminent loss of money or status'. Once such a fear is kindled, change becomes possible; possible because now it's vital.

Experts in change management know this. They know that for change to take place there has to be a 'burning platform'. Unfortunately, this tends to manifest itself as a 'case for change', a set of logical arguments designed to persuade people of the rationale for doing things differently. It's unfortunate because a case for change converts the emotional heat of the burning platform into something far cooler and intellectual: it turns fire into air.

The burning-platform approach comes down to scaring people into change. But there is another appeal to be made, an appeal less frightening than burning platforms and more emotional than the rational 'case for change'. The appeal in this case is to the human truth that you have to change in order to grow. At some level all individuals and organisations harbour this deep desire for growth, for development. Suppressing it seems to go against nature.

To illustrate the point, I'll finish with a quick cautionary tale about a Saudi company I once advised. It was in the business of bidding for and, when successful, delivering government contracts to get the rising number of unemployed into work. At the same time, however, the country was beginning to experience a skills shortage, especially in the service sector. With the oil set to run out, the in this case literal burning platforms could not go on burning for ever, so the long-term future of the country depended on that service sector expanding to compensate. As it happens, there were plenty of people keen to be trained and employed in that sector, but these people were female, and women weren't supposed to work. The economy was suffering, the women were suffering, but change was a bridge too far. So how would Saudi Arabia grow in the future, both economically and socially, without embracing such a critical change? For a country that's been as rich as it has, the prospect of any change at all is disconcerting. But inevitably that change will come; it's just a question of how long you're prepared to suffer in the meantime.

# 9

# DO YOU LOVE MONEY?

Yesterday I listened to a podcast about the Quakers. The programme focused on their religious beliefs, but near the end it pointed out how successful they had been – and continue to be – in business. Is that not a contradiction? I wondered. Can you be religious and make money? What is an appropriate relationship to money for someone religious who runs a business? And are atheists off the hook? Are they free to pursue as much wealth as their hearts desire? Of course, money is business's lifeblood, and generally speaking we do measure business success in monetary terms, but it's a bit more complicated than that, regardless of one's religious stance.

There are psychological factors, for example. Plenty of people are in business to make money, but run up against mental barriers. They undercharge because they don't want to appear greedy, and so lose out; or they overcharge, because they are, and then lose custom or trust. The law firm I mentioned in the Preface would annually set its sights on significantly raised revenue uplift for the following year, but were too gentlemanly to chase the revenue down. Again, the tension between strategy and reality was abundantly clear.

So how best in a business to manage one's attitude to money, in order to be successful without being vilified? So that money is indeed lifeblood and not toxin?

According to the proverb, the love of money is the root of all evil. If most people are in business to make money, it implies that money is something they at least like, perhaps even love. But does it follow that there's something fundamentally evil about being in business?

To a militant mindset, the answer of course is yes. Business aims to produce a profit mostly retained by the owners. This private squirrelling away of money leads to disparities in wealth and associated inequalities. So in effect, business is about prospering at someone else's expense, creating a society in which the good life of the few is bought at the cost of a bad life for the many. That is 'evil', possibly not in the religious sense, but certainly in the social one.

The non-militant majority, as we know, hold a different view. Without business, they say, there is neither wealth creation nor progress. Money is a great motivator that gets people making the products and offering the services that other people want. The result is that quality of life improves all round. Those other people might even discover the employment they might not otherwise have found, in that very enterprise. If the owners of such enterprises end up making a profit, that is their just reward for taking a risk on an idea, and then working hard to make it happen. Money makes the world go around.

Either way, we don't tend to ask people if they love money, however familiar the proverb. In fact, we're squeamish about money questions generally, a phenomenon no doubt due to capitalism itself. Consider: in a communist society, where everyone earns the same (in theory, at least), we don't need to ask because it's not interesting. In the capitalist version, with its inherent variations in wealth, it becomes very interesting indeed, yet paradoxically the variations themselves make the subject too sensitive to probe.

I was once involved in developing an idea for a TV show

whose drama consisted in the workers in a business finding out how much each other earned. As the discoveries were made and the discrepancies exposed, a great taboo was broken, the resulting emotions running the gamut from guilty smugness to frothing outrage. The key assumption on which the drama appeared to turn was that money is intrinsically desirable. The TV show couldn't have said it more clearly. And yet it wasn't the money per se that was the issue. It was the unevenness in how it had been distributed – the variations again. The money could have been replaced by apples or even abstract symbols. What the TV show really exposed was how deep in us the instinct for fairness runs. Although we might assent quite readily to the concept of capitalism, when we find out how far down the pecking order we really are, it can seem like the worst idea in the world.

So when it comes to loving money, what are the options? To pretend not to love it, while secretly craving more? Obviously not. One of my most interesting clients was a billionaire who made his fortune by investing in various capital-intensive businesses, from shipbuilding to mining. What I learned from him is that when it comes to the love of money, there is the appropriate and there is the inappropriate kind. The latter is apparent in many of the people who solicit him for invest-ment funds. Essentially, they see money as a short cut. It's as if they are thinking, 'If we just had more money, we'd get to where we want to get to much quicker, and then relax.' The return they have to pay to their angel, the billionaire, is effec-tively the price of time and effort saved.

The appropriate kind, by contrast, sees money as what enables the work to happen. You love money appropriately when you see it as the resource that allows you to rent the workshop where you'll restore antiques, or fund the research you've wanted to do on ageing, or open a hotel. The money in such cases is not about sparing you some effort but about filling your tank at the start of a journey.

# 10

# HOW MUCH IS ENOUGH?

As we all know, Richard Branson started by selling indie records from a telephone box. He was the upstart entrepreneur ready to take on the big guys, a David to many Goliaths. And since David won, he became in the UK something of a national treasure, knighted by the Queen.

But there is a shadow side. Less remarked upon is that, as a consequence of his whizz-kid zeal, his Virgin empire grew to dimensions as colossal as any of the corporates he was staking out. The portfolio included major airlines and railway companies, and it made its founding father sufficiently wealthy to buy himself a Caribbean island. He didn't wish just to open up the market by challenging the monopolies that had more than their fair share – as if, with his beard and jumper, he were a kind of socialist capitalist. No: Branson needed to be the new giant on the block, and all the lobbying against monopolies was designed to make it easier for him to attain that goal. He challenged monopolies so that he could become one. David became Goliath.

I paint this unflattering portrait, so at variance with the public Branson profile, in order to identify what counts in a business as enough. It's a question too few leaders ask, one consequence being that their strategies amount to little more than desires to grow, to do better this year than last. Although at first sight it seems like the Branson ambition is similarly to keep on growing, the growth has a significant, but easily missed, cap. Enough, for Branson, is to displace and preferably usurp the dominant player in a given market. His method is a serial assassination of bogeymen so that he can step into their shoes, becoming that Goliath. Once that's done, a new market – anything from wedding dresses to wine – may be sought out by a reincarnated David, until he becomes Goliath again. And so on.

The Branson example points to something more singular and intense than the impossible pursuit of more. As does that of the English lord for whom I once did a small piece of consultancy. He was the latest in a noble line stretching back centuries, and his most heartfelt ambition was to maintain the estate he had inherited – stately home, grounds, the local town and its houses, artworks, investments and so on – in such a way that both line and estate should continue after his death. Enough, for him, was preservation. Again, this enough was singular, intense – and very personal.

But new-money knights and old-money lords are scarcely the norm. What about businesses of a less exotic nature? What if you're running an architect's practice, a shipping agency, a textile factory or a chain of restaurants? Typically, the question of enough never gets asked, certainly not when it comes to producing strategy. Instead, a financial target gets set, and set without its setters really asking why. All too often it's based merely on the best that can be achieved under prevailing market conditions and with the resource anticipated to deliver it. Sure, everyone would prefer more money, but this ambition just doesn't have the sharpness a business decision demands. Think how much clarity would be brought to the strategy if the first question in producing it was: 'How much is enough?' That would focus the mind. It would introduce something bracingly real.

It does occasionally happen, of course, and with surprising results. I remember pitching for (and not winning) a project with a European bank embarrassed by its record on customer service, a record mercilessly paraded by the newspapers. I naïvely assumed they hoped to turn things around, to show their customers how good they could be. But all they wanted was enough of an improvement in satisfaction scores to staunch the flow of bad publicity. 'Help us to be average,' was the message. That would be enough.

Not exactly thrilling as a strategy (or as a consulting project), but at least they were being honest. Not to mention they were giving more weight to reality than strategy, an approach I can only endorse. It was enough for them to provide average customer service, because doing more would be too costly: the strictly regulated number of minutes a call-centre operative was allowed to deal with a customer would have to increase, and to make their Internet service anything like user-friendly would require major surgery. Being a volume provider, they weren't prepared to erode already tight margins with such expensive upgrades. The point was to do 'just enough' on customer service to get the press off their back, and make sure there was still revenue rolling in overall. Perhaps those who assume 'customer service' to be a panacea can learn a lesson here: the company's volume customers were only paying a small amount for their service, and the service they received was no more or less than what was in proportion. Why serve your customers in excess of what they pay you?

I had previously done a project with a similar feel, for another financial services firm. The brief was to delayer the upper echelons of the organisation chart. There were too many senior managers, with too many overlaps between them and not enough 'height' between layers. My colleagues and I designed what we considered an elegant solution, which made sure that (a) there was reasonable space between one job and those above and below it, and (b) management spans weren't luxuriously narrow. Had they taken on board our recommendations, they would have saved a significant amount of money. But they didn't, and my surmise remains that they simply had enough money already, and didn't need any more. Way too many senior staff there may have been all drawing handsome salaries, but the bank could comfortably wear it. To go ahead and implement the delayering exercise they had called for seemed like unnecessary graft. Enough, in their case, really was enough.

In sum, the question 'How much is enough?' bridges the gap between the fantasy of strategy and the facts of reality. It gives a truer mark of the ambition to run against than the typical strategy question which is essentially 'How much do we want?', and which is too open-ended to be useful. It also gets at both corporate and individual aspirations, because it prompts the business to think in real terms about the time it would take to get enough, and it forces individuals to weigh up their own financial needs.

# 11

# WHAT DISASTERS ARE BEING BORN AS YOU READ THIS?

I first came across the name Osama Bin Laden about a year before 9/11. It was in a document I had been granted permission to consult by a then client of mine in the British government. The document comprised an analysis of defence threats to the United Kingdom. Bin Laden was clearly identified as hostile. As I was reading about him, the man himself would have already conceived and begun planning the attack that made him known to a world well beyond experts in defence.

Like pretty much everyone else, I had no idea of the disaster being born as I read about him. In fact, what struck me most was that the document began not with the military or even the political landscape, but with water. Long term, it was climate change and its effects on the availability of water, forcing migration from barren to fertile areas of the planet, that were most likely to cause the greatest tension. Competition for resources would increase, borders would become jealously guarded, and food prices would change the shape of the economy. Under such circumstances, nation states would get jumpy and belligerent.

At about the same time, I heard the story of a friend's friend, an independent investor. I was told that he was buying up vast tracts of cheap land in the Australian outback.

Naturally I asked why. 'Two reasons,' said my friend. 'First, because he says the levels of borrowing we're seeing in the West are unsustainable. Although we're all obsessed with the knowledge economy, there'll come a time when the value of real goods becomes greater again. Australia has huge reserves of mineral wealth. Second, because China will become more affluent, and as it becomes more affluent, diets will change. Chinese people will want to eat beef. Beef comes from cattle, and cattle need land. He's going to meet the demand from Australia.'

What I've just related are two examples of strategy: military strategy and investment strategy. And what they have in common is that they're far longer term than most strategies in the world of company business. Needless to say, that doesn't apply to all businesses. Two of my former clients were Northrop Grumman and BAE, both defence contractors. They build warships, drones, jets, helicopters and aircraft carriers. In a way, 'business strategy' is irrelevant to them, because their timescales fall well beyond what a normal business cycle could encompass. I'm reliably informed that building an aircraft carrier can take anything up to fifteen years. Not just because of the production process involved in such a large-scale effort but because agreeing the contract and the specification is so momentous. As a Western company, hypothetically speaking, you might agree to build fighter jets for a Libyan company, only for the latter to become an object of public loathing in the aftermath of the Arab Spring.

So some companies are 'strategic' by default. The scale of their operation and the political implications are such that a business decision has to be taken in the context of both a wider world and a longer time horizon. Such examples suggest that everything happening in your business today is a symptom of something far larger. Not long ago, for example, the UK music and film retailer HMV went into administration. It couldn't compete with Internet sales, and so it caved in to the inevitable. This disaster could have been foreseen several years ago. Sometimes it's only by zooming out to that bigger picture that you can begin to pick up the disasters being born as you merrily carry on.

Alongside the threats, of course, are opportunities. The case of HMV and others leads us to think that the Internet is killing the high street, but these are merely the effects of something that was set in train a fair time ago. The question now, therefore, is not how to save certain high-street retailers, it's to reconceive what the 'high street' might be about in the future, and what opportunities will open up. A good question might be: 'What's the high street for?' That leads you to all sorts of long-term issues. Because if the high street is full of shops that people don't shop in any more, perhaps it will die, and shops will continue to close, like churches and pubs have continued to close. And yet shops, churches and pubs all provide something extra to their core offer of goods, religion or booze – they all provide a place to congregate and look at other people. So is that the longer-term opportunity? Can we avoid the disasters that have affected these various institutions by looking much more closely at what's really behind them?

Or consider the American insurance company I was with last week. They were bemoaning the decline in revenue from the automotive sector. As cars become more reliable, insurance spend goes down. They were pretty gloomy about their life insurance business too, and for not dissimilar reasons: people are living longer and healthcare is improving. So I got them to step back and ask themselves, 'Is the world getting riskier?' The answer came back as a resounding 'Yes!'. Politically, economically and socially, instability lies all around; the growth of global interconnectivity means that predicting patterns of behaviour becomes intensely more difficult. My follow-up question was: 'So if the world is getting riskier, there's more opportunity for a firm that sells insurance?' After a pause, another big yes. Instead of giving in to the 'disaster' of falling revenue in the automotive and life sectors, they had a golden opportunity to take advantage of long-term trends – but only if they began by recognising who they were and that their core business was not 'auto' or 'life' per se, but protection against risk.

Almost certainly there are disasters being born as you read this. Your own business might become a victim of them. But equally, if you lay your conventional 'strategy' aside for a moment and consider instead the reality of longer-term trends, and the clues they offer to the entrepreneur, you may be OK.

# 12

# WHAT ARE THE UNINTENDED CONSEQUENCES?

One side effect of the obsession with strategy as commonly conceived is that it restricts the vision of the organisation in question to the market. It frames organisations as purely commercial entities. We know they are more than that. Just as all organisations leave an environmental footprint on the planet, they also make a social footprint in the world. They are places where people go to work, where they spend the majority of their waking lives, where they form relationships. Because they are also places from which those people draw money in exchange for their labour, livelihoods are at stake. A client just told me about the business he ran in a former life, employing 120 people. 'Those were 120 mortgages I was supporting,' he reflected.

Large consumer-facing businesses – Walmart, say – have a status in the mind of those consumers that goes beyond the need for groceries. They are landmarks, not in the same way that a temple or a bridge might be a landmark, but as points of reference around which everyday life will orient itself. They represent a force in shaping social behaviour.

And there are those companies – I'm thinking of the ones that operate nuclear power plants – whose societal presence actually looms larger than any commercial facet. To the popular mind it's almost a jolt to be reminded that they need to make money, so prominent is the issue of safety, so terrifying the potential danger they contain. The 'business leader' of a site that enriches uranium may well be – may well have to be – a businessman or a businesswoman, but it's hardly this profile with which we're concerned. The role is much more serious than that. They are nothing less than the watchmen entrusted with preventing apocalypse.

The same applies in less high-stake contexts. Generally it takes a scandal to remind us of the non-strategy aspects of an organisation that are nevertheless always there. Think of the story that broke some years ago about Nike and the atrocious conditions at certain of its factories. At such moments, we consumers get an unexpected glimpse into the wider ecology of the organisation we habitually view with blinkers. But even where the workers aren't being exploited, the surrounding ecology remains. The business that goes on in a business ramifies way beyond the organisation, out into the real world.

One of the factors that stops us all (not just business leaders) from maintaining this more holistic perspective is what I would term the 'myth of outsourcing'. As I write this chapter in my study at home on a snowy day in south London, I hear the gritter rumble past. I dart to the window just in time to observe the vehicle. It is marked 'Conway'. Conway must have been contracted by my local council to spread the salt. For the council, it is no doubt cheaper than doing it in-house. For me, not only does my road become less hazardous, I'm implicitly saved a bit of council tax. As for Conway, it's a contract won. Good news all round, or a 'win/win/win' as a consultant might say.

But even under an outsourcing arrangement, you remain in relationship, and responsibility isn't entirely devolved. Say the gritter slid on the snow it was about to treat, and it knocked someone over. Neither Conway nor the council could rightly absent themselves from facing the music. To whatever respective degrees, they're in it together. In business, we sit within a very long chain of consequences from which we can't simply detach ourselves, a fact that digital technology is making increasingly hard to ignore. Before too long, the sweatshop you choose to run in the Philippines will appear in a photo on Twitter; the farmers you bargained into poverty will out you on Facebook; and on TripAdvisor the guests you fleeced will take their revenge.

In other words, the holistic view I'm describing might sound like an ethical option to be chosen, as if you could equally choose not to make it, but in truth the option is being inexorably withdrawn. Business leaders have got used to the idea of being under scrutiny from staff, from shareholders, from customers. But they're only just waking up to their visibility to the entire ecosystem whose centre they occupy. Better, therefore, to start thinking early about the wider consequences, and make sure they are the ones that were intended.

# PART 2

# IN THE MARKET

# INTRODUCTION

This second part narrows in on the market. But I'm not offering market analysis along the lines of Michael E. Porter's five forces with its 'barriers to entry' and so on. You can do your market analysis and still find that the market refuses to behave in the way your analysis said it should. Reality intervenes in the shape of customers who are more complex than your Client Relationship Management (CRM) software allowed. It intervenes in the shape of competitors you never saw coming. It intervenes in the shape of innovations that change the market for everyone.

But none of this means having to despair. Rather it means factoring in this unpredictable reality from the start – dealing with the fact that uncertainty is an essential part of leading a business, not an aberration.

Take heart in this: if the market were entirely predictable, programmed to play out along foreseeable lines, influencing it would not be possible. The inherent uncertainty of the market means you can exert influence. And the best way to influence it is for your profile to be as unique, human and attractive as possible. To be sure, there's often plenty of business to be had by replicating what others in your sector do. But if you want to call yourself a business leader, as opposed to a manager, you can't rely on copying others.

One of the key assumptions to overcome in all this is that

how you are on the inside as a business won't affect how you are on the outside. It's a theme that will come up in various ways in this section. The digital access that people have to companies means those companies are becoming more and more transparent, which is making it harder for any branding to disguise the reality. In this sense, the market doesn't begin outside the front door, but inside the boardroom.

# 13

# IS YOUR BUSINESS
# AN ONLY CHILD?

In the autumn of 2012, the *Economist* ran an article about the demise of Monitor, a management consultancy firm. With my professional interest in the industry, I naturally read it:

Monitor had seen bright days. It was founded by six partners with close ties to Harvard in 1983. One of them, Michael Porter, is one of few who can legitimately claim the title of a legendary business guru. Over the years, Monitor was able to compete with the likes of much bigger McKinsey, the Boston Consulting Group and Bain, for top graduates, whom it offered an almost academic image and cachet.

But the recession was hard on the firm. As the economy nosedived after 2008, few companies shelled out for pure strategy consulting. Meanwhile, the top-tier firms had long since begun to push into operations as well as strategy, and so went on being hired as companies sought help getting lean. That, plus their sheer size, helped the top-tier consultants ride out the storm. Monitor was not so lucky; pure advisory consulting took years to recover, as economic uncertainty kept companies sitting on their plans (and cash) for taking over the world.

I knew Monitor a little bit from the inside, through friends who worked there; and though this isn't a scientific statement, I can safely say that from what I saw it had something special. As the *Economist* notes, there was an 'almost academic' atmosphere, but this didn't mean it wasn't focused on helping its clients achieve their commercial objectives. Perhaps that was what was unique: the blending of otherwise contradictory characteristics, ivory-tower thinking and hard-nosed advice. More philosophical than an accountancy firm, but more savvy than a business school, it seemed one of a kind. An only child, perhaps.

The *Economist* rightly points out, however, that Monitor was not alone in its middle-weight class (1,200 consultants worldwide compared with over 7,000 at McKinsey). Citing Tom Rodenhauser of Kennedy Information, it notes that:

> AT Kearney and Booz & Company, for example, considered merging several years ago, a union that many observers thought was born of weakness. Small specialist firms have loyal clients and fewer costs. Mid-tier firms try to maintain a global footprint of offices and top-shelf brands, but cannot deliver 50 experienced consultants on short notice.

So Monitor was not an only child, but a middle child (like AT Kearney and Booz), stuck between the big boys and the boutiques. Holding the middle course was always going to be tricky when the economy took a sudden lurch towards a ditch.

Nevertheless, I maintain that Monitor was special in an only-child kind of way – not due to its size so much as the unique feel it had. Despite its fall, it had an aura, and an aura is no ordinary commodity. The question is whether an aura is any use. To put it bluntly, will a 'special' organisation fare better in the market?

Many of us will have had the experience, if only once or twice, of coming together with a group of people and feeling there was a certain magic to it. Maybe it was the sports team we were a member of, which seemed to operate on telepathic understanding. Maybe it was the days we spent on a residential course, during which a bond developed among the participants that would have been hard to explain to the outside world. Maybe it was a project we developed in our business, when there was a sense of flow in the work and a fluidity among those involved. Just occasionally, the planets seem to align, and something extraordinary connects those in a given system at a given time.

It sounds wonderful, does it not? It's possible that you, as a business leader, wish your own organisation had a bit more of this X factor. But the glaring problem with it, as in the case of Monitor, is that a warm glow on the inside doesn't always translate into success in the commercial world. The fellow-feeling among the staff has to be channelled into delivering the company's market ambitions, and if it isn't, it's just self-indulgence.

To illustrate the point, I'll mention a series of Constellations I ran for a major corporate client. By 'Constellations' I mean a technique that literally maps out the issues in a business, so that you get a spatial picture of where the blockages are – the twist being that this map is not drawn on paper, but acted out live, using human beings to represent the various elements. My corporate client was very keen that its strategy, which was to penetrate emerging markets, was clearly understood and actively embraced by everyone in the organisation, so what we mapped in the Constellation were a) the strategy, and b) the various business units. We wanted to look at the relationship between the two, to see how prominently the strategy actually registered in the minds of those charged with its implementation.

What we found was that not only was the link between each business unit and the strategy weak, but that other links were much stronger. People were less attached to the strategy than to each other. Like a spaceship inside which there's a party going on and only one poor soul at the helm, the internal relationships easily attracted more attention and energy than the direction of the company. Perhaps shockingly, we also discovered that people were more attached to the physical place they worked in – the office at which they were based – than they were to any overarching corporate imperative.

This is absolutely where most of the connecting energy in an organisation goes. People connect to each other before they connect to the larger purpose of succeeding in the market. Small wonder that getting people, except perhaps those at the most senior level, to properly engage in strategy is often an uphill struggle. Strategy makes for a lot feebler an attractor of people than other people. No sooner have you hired someone to help implement your strategy than they meet their co-workers and form relationships that will loom much larger in their working lives. Sometimes they will also connect to the company's customers, but again it's a connection that tends to come before the strategy of the enterprise that employs them. Such bonding might not always attain the magical levels I described a moment ago, but the instincts that point in that direction are strong.

All this is pretty sobering if you consider the primary purpose of a business is to be effective in the market rather than facilitate human bonding. The question therefore for a business leader is how to turn this bonding between employees into competitive advantage (as opposed to stamping on it).

The first task is to actually observe where the strongest relationships lie, and where possible to organise work around them. After all, the energy present in a strong human relationship can be a huge asset in terms of getting work done. Conversely, think of the problems that sometimes arise when people who don't like each other are forced to work cheek by jowl: the work can often suffer. However, because the positive relationships don't always fall within organisational boxes – people like people outside their own team – you have to look for projects where they can collaborate across their normal team lines.

For me, this is a good example of tempering strategy with reality. Too many businesses will simply establish a strategy and parcel it out to the relevant organisational units to deliver, regardless of the reality of the human relationships within and across those units. It's as if the quality of those relationships can have no impact on the quality of the product/service experienced by the customer. But how can it not? The moral is to work with the reality of the relationships and use it to the advantage of the business. It's a question of directing that energy to best effect.

## 14

# IS YOUR BRAND A MASK OR A WINDOW?

Recently I was looking to buy a new car, and had narrowed it down to a BMW or a Skoda. Chalk and cheese, you might think. The 'ultimate driving machine' versus a vehicle whose brand history was – how shall I put it? – chequered. Old joke:

'How do you double the value of a Skoda?'

'Fill up the tank.'

Since Skoda Auto was acquired by Volkswagen, however, things have drastically improved, so much so that these days Skodas are less likely to pick up a wise remark than a motoring award. Reader, I bought the Skoda.

But during the buying process it was that brand issue that vexed me most. On paper, the Skoda was as good as the BMW in almost every department, and better in some. Because what counts as an extra on the German vehicle comes as standard on the Czech, it was also about 30 per cent cheaper. Yet I was worried what the brand would say about me. More precisely, what my friends would say, what the other parents in the school car park would say, what my clients would say. And now I'm worried what my readers will say.

It's just such anxiety that is picked up in an article in the *McKinsey Quarterly*. This emotional space of the brand is where competitive leverage can be found, and therefore it's what should be vexing the car manufacturers too:

> In recent years, the number of car makes and models has grown in every product segment. At the same time, the once vast gaps in quality, performance, safety, fuel efficiency, and amenities have all closed significantly. Although variations in quality and performance persist, the remaining possibilities for differentiating products, and thus achieving competitive advantage, revolve around styling and other intangibles and the emotional benefits they confer on the customer. But instead of attempting to convey these benefits, carmakers spend 55 percent of their marketing budgets – $24 billion a year – on rebates and incentives.

What I felt about the BMW was that it had actually achieved what the article was recommending. Apart from contributing to the cost of the glitzy showroom on Park Lane where I went for my test drive, that 30 per cent differential was the price of my emotions. The implicit calculation BMW were making was that I would spend about that much extra, not to have a better car, but to feel better about myself. So why didn't I buy it? I saw through the marketing. And having seen through it, I felt not better, but worse. The BMW brand, I felt, existed to mask the fact that the car didn't justify the premium. Beneath the thrill at the prospect of owning a new BMW ran the disquieting sensation that I was being ripped off.

The Skoda showroom, near the ring road in Oxford, is so chock-a-block with cars on its meagre forecourt that even finding the front door requires some initiative. The space itself is dated and the customer toilets far from de luxe. But the car I drove was superb, literally – a Skoda Superb. A tough billing to live up to, but between the brand name and the reality there really wasn't much difference, as if the brand were a window. Yes, the BMW had been superb too, superb and arrogant. This Skoda was superb and modest. Little manipulation of my feelings was involved, just excellent value for money.

Which is perhaps the alternative conclusion to the premise of the *McKinsey Quarterly* article. It argues that because cars are all becoming the same, the only way to differentiate is through the brand; I've heard the same argument applied to supermarkets. But you could argue just as convincingly that all other things being equal, what will win the day is price. Why not save on branding and offer the same quality cars for less money? We might think in a very modern way that brand value is the only way forward, all other sources of value having been maxed out, but it ain't necessarily so. Equally, you could say that if all cars are achieving similar levels of competence, true competitive advantage lies in a step-change in quality. The diesel engine in the BMW that I drove, for example, might have been smooth, powerful and responsive, but it also rattled like a tractor. Take its brand away, and to compete BMW would have to offer a car that is demonstrably 30 per cent better than the Skoda, across every measure – 'quality, performance, safety, fuel efficiency, and amenities'.

This argument about brands goes well beyond cars, of course. Price and quality will usually be more decisive for a customer than brand. After all, brand is principally a means of disguising or at least artificially enhancing the reality behind it, and if the brand gets too far ahead of that reality, consumer confidence in it will start to break down, and vice versa. Of course, a brand will never offer a comprehensive picture of the product or service it represents, but it should at least be a focused presentation of reality, not a strategic distortion of it. To use an obvious example, Apple became the world's largest company not only because its brand was hugely desirable, but because of the quality and price of its products. Expensive, yes, but you get what you pay for. Which is how someone like me can own both an iPhone and a Skoda Superb, but not a BMW.

So why is this an important question for business leaders? Because in any given organisation it's only the boss who has as rounded a view of the company product or proposition as the customer. Beneath the boss, people will push their own agenda, the brand guys pushing the brand, the designers pushing the design, the engineers pushing the technology, and so on. It's only the boss who can take a non-partisan view of the whole. It's this whole that the customer sees, making boss and customer kind of equivalents on opposite sides of the counter. One of the leader's key roles, in other words, is ensuring that the brand is less of a mask and more of a window.

# 15

# WHAT ARE YOUR PHEROMONES?

The car has picked me up from Brussels airport, and I am en route, under a grey sky, to the NATO headquarters on the city's outskirts. My purpose for being here is to run a disaster-planning exercise for a senior British diplomat and his team. In the preceding few weeks I have, under strict conditions, been scanning through classified documents in the Foreign Office and the Ministry of Defence in London, to look at scenarios developed by strategists in the two departments. Today, we're going to see how the NATO Brussels operation might react to a specific scenario we have focused on. We've chosen it because it satisfies our two main criteria: likelihood of happening and gravity of impact.

The NATO compound is set back from the main road behind a perimeter fence. The security process to get in is lengthy. Armed guards look on with humourless expressions. In my suit and tie, I'm suddenly conscious of the term 'civilian': I feel like a lightweight. Finally, we're in.

Even if you had no idea what the buildings were that lay behind the fence, your body would have done the knowing for you. The whole place gives off a powerful sense of what it is – its pheromones, if you will. There's no mistaking the seriousness of its function, and as I approach it's a strange mixture of safety and danger that I feel in my gut.

Contrast that with an experience that was pretty much the opposite. It's some years later and I'm at the offices of Ingenious Media, on Golden Square in London's Soho. In the sunny square, thirty-somethings with coffees and casual designer clothes are holding impromptu meetings around iPads, retro scooters are circling, and the queue for the organic deli stretches out the door.

In reception, I'm greeted with a smile from a young woman who's so pretty and so well put together she could be a model, and I'm shown across a reflective floor, past various artworks and a door that opens on a bar, to a leather banquette, to wait for my host and sip the sparkling water I've been handed. Occasionally, handsome young men with trimmed beards walk by and acknowledge me warmly. It's so like being in a boutique five-star hotel that I almost forget I'm here for a meeting.

I draw this contrast not to emphasise the diversity of working life as a consultant, though the diversity is real. In fact, I don't want to draw the contrast at all. I want to emphasise not how different the two experiences were, but how similar. For in both cases, it was the intensity of the 'pheromones' that counted. Both operations knew exactly what they were about and weren't afraid of projecting it. One was in the international security business and made no bones about being so. The other inhabited the gilded world of the media, and was glad to make the fact emphatically clear.

The effect on me of their confidence in their own identity was in both cases to draw me into their world, even before I'd had a chance to process it. From the moment I entered their airspace, so to speak, I found myself unequivocally captured and doing business on their terms. It probably altered my behaviour too: pathetically trying to act more macho at

NATO, more cool in Soho. It wasn't that I was on the back foot, exactly, or that I was suddenly deprived of my own inner resources. It was more that the intense specificity or singularity of each place acted like a body of heavy mass on another body of lighter mass: each pulled me into its orbit. It really was physical.

You might dismiss what I'm describing as 'brand', as in, both the NATO brand and the Ingenious Media brand were strong enough to have an impact on me. But it was deeper than that. This was about the inner identity of an organisation being expressed in so pure and unfiltered a way that as a visitor I felt I was being dipped into a different liquid, immersed in a different atmosphere. It's the equivalent, perhaps, of entering a medieval church: whether you're a believer or not, the whole feel of the place takes you into another, highly particular realm.

So my point is exactly that brand is superficial, and that the 'pheromonal' identity I'm describing carries a far heftier punch. The contrast I would make is with the many organisations whose identity is so insipid that it's hard to tell one from another. Without naming names, I'll offer just one example.

On a business trip to Tokyo, I found myself at the headquarters of one of the country's most iconic companies. As it was my first meeting with them, I arrived in a state of some excitement. But the excitement began to dispel before I'd even got inside. The building was unexceptional, unmarked and hard to find. The reception area could not have been more generic, and the office in which my meeting was held could have been in any city in the corporate world. Despite the company's fame, what it projected to the outside world was utterly lacking in character (unlike some other Japanese companies I know).

The meeting passed off with reasonable success, but I was left with the impression of having been left with no impression. For all its weight in the world, this was a company lacking the kind of pheromones I'm describing. Perhaps this lack of impression is not unrelated to the fact that the company, though still an icon, is no longer the power it once was. A day later, I noticed I was markedly less enthused about following up with them, even though the business opportunity I was pursuing with them was far from insignificant.

Companies aren't solely commercial entities. They're social, environmental, symbolic. This means we experience them on all sorts of levels, one of which is the deeper 'pheromonal' level that can be felt in the body. Those companies who pay attention to this level can have a far greater impact. They can bring people into their world-view in a way that a brand can barely touch. It's not necessarily to do with putting everything on show, as the NATO case demonstrates, because the 'pheromones' in their case had a lot to do with secrecy and security. It's more about being bold in projecting who you are and what's different about you.

# 16

# WOULD YOU BUY
# WHAT YOU SELL?

In 1949, the firm of Rowland Smith & Son, managed by Messrs. R. W. Smith and R. R. Smith, imported various products into Great Britain under their brand Ye Olde Oak. After years of rationing during World War II, the people started to desire quality and new ideas for meals again. The reputation of Ye Olde Oak grew fast and it became synonymous with products of consistently high quality … At the beginning of the 1960s, Ye Olde Oak was the largest brand in Great Britain. This was due to the large success of the remarkable pear-formed ham. In this period, Ye Olde Oak was prominent in the development of advertising in Great Britain. Ye Olde Oak invested considerably in publicity and was the first food product company to use radio and television advertising. It was also among the first brands that manifested itself with a great illuminated advertisement at Piccadilly Circus in London.

The text above is taken from the website of Ye Olde Oak, which is a division of Struik Foods Europe. As you'll have guessed, it has personal significance for me. R. W. Smith was my grandfather, and R. R. Smith was his brother, the great-uncle Robert Rowland Smith after whom I was named. My father, Colin Rowland Smith, also worked for the family business. During his tenure, he'd bring home tins of the famous ham, and we'd dutifully consume it for Sunday supper. In the 1970s, the time I'm speaking of, when I was a boy, tinned ham was still ever so slightly upmarket, even if today the reverse is true. Although some people complained about the savoury jelly in which the 'pear-formed' meat was embalmed, the ham was fairly tasty. Would we have bought it, however, if my dad hadn't got it for free? Possibly not.

This raises the question of whether you'd buy what you sell – 'eating your own dog food', as computer companies say – and the degree to which you stand by what you're putting out to the market. Of course, there are limits. If you're in medical prosthetics, for instance, the chances are you'll be making only so many purchases on your own behalf. But the issue of believing in your stuff, whether you buy it or not, might nevertheless be pretty significant because it's something customers can generally pick up on. Do you have a passion for your business, or does it just help pay the rent?

When, after ten years lecturing at Oxford, I went into business myself, I found myself helping to run a firm whose original strap-line had been 'Passion Purpose Performance'. The theory behind the phrase can be explained as follows.

Probably the most widely held belief about how business works is that you first decide on what you're going to do, and then you do it. Strategy followed by implementation. It's a highly rational approach, and you will have seen it repre-sented in a thousand different versions by an arrow on a PowerPoint slide going from left to right. Plan > Do. In terms of the 'p' words above, you have a purpose, and that purpose gets executed more or less well according to the company's overall performance.

The fly in this otherwise commendable ointment is precisely

that performance can vary hugely. Even the best strategy in the world can be fluffed when it comes to executing it (this is one of the more obvious reasons why the obsession in business with strategy is unhealthy). So how do you control performance?

Again there are classic rational answers. These typically come down to tightening up processes or restructuring the organisation chart. Both approaches can indeed yield benefit, although as we all know, organisational restructuring tends to be much more about politics or power than about performance. We also know, then, that structures need people to populate them just as processes require people to work them. Maybe one day it will exist, but at the time of writing, a business with zero people is not something I've encountered.

And when it comes to people and controlling their performance, the classic answer in that case is to set targets. If you're a lawyer, I give you a monthly fee-earning target; a travelling salesman, I give you a weekly target of units sold; a train driver, I set you a target for punctuality. And then I pay you. As a leader I can add up all the actual figures attained against the targets I set, and the result is the overall performance of the company.

But that gap between target figure and actual figure is pivotal. Essentially, it's where the discretionary energy of the people working for you is locked up – the 'extra mile' that people might be able to go. In effect this extra mile represents the focus of pretty much the whole art of leadership, because it gets at how to make your business more productive. After all, you don't really need any leaders as such if performance against target, both individual and corporate, is unvaryingly spot on. Even where you can get people to perform consistently, there will be collateral costs, the classic example being the call centre in which people are forced to answer a prescribed number of calls, but sickness absence is high; i.e. when people are there they perform consistently, but the level of consistent performance means they're not always there. That translates as an imperative for a different kind of leadership, one that treats people not simply as units of production, but as naturally variable beings whose variability is a real business factor to be built into the leader's considerations, as opposed to an anomaly to be expunged. 'Passion' therefore is short-hand for the expenditure of discretionary energy, the amount of give from your people that is available to you as a leader.

How does all this help to answer the question of whether you'd buy what you sell? Well, a passion for the product isn't really possible unless the answer to the question is yes. And why is a passion for the product good? Because the customer can feel it. That person in the call centre is a whole lot more convincing to the customer on the phone line when she or he is reasonably engaged in what they're talking about. OK, maybe 'passion' is too strong a word, but a palpable lack of passion is what as a customer you all too often get. And as a leader, that means you want to home in on the discretionary energy that might be available to you and your business. When you're out of rational answers, it can help close the gap in performance, and bring you closer to your customers.

# 17

# ARE YOUR CUSTOMERS AS REAL AS YOU ARE?

A market is filled with buyers and sellers, and between the two lies the dividing line that sets them apart. In an actual market, this dividing line is represented by the table on which are piled the goods for sale – fruit and vegetables, for instance, or cheap jewellery. My first ever holiday job was working in a market like this, selling cheese. I would cut wedges of Cheddar or Stilton using a cheese wire, package them in waxed paper, hand them to the customer, receive their notes and give them their change. What struck me most was how different it was being on this side of the table, selling, compared to being on the other side, buying. People loom up at you out of a sea of faces, look dispassionately at what you have to offer, not necessarily making eye contact, ask for what they want in a matter-of-fact way, and make the exchange before moving off without ceremony. They seem very different from how they appear when you're rubbing alongside them, on the other side of the table, a buyer among buyers. It's a little alienating.

In other words, something quite profound happens when we cross the dividing line between buyer and seller, and go stand behind the table. Suddenly it's harder to see things from the customer's perspective, even though you've been a customer yourself right up until that point. Perhaps it's because as a seller you feel a bit exposed, a bit judged, so your instinct is to protect yourself rather than put yourself in the shoes of the customer on the other side of the table. Very soon you the seller see the buyers as an undifferentiated 'Joe Public', and that table between you and them serves not just as a commercial platform but as an emotional buffer.

I'd argue that it's in the face of this fundamental separation between buyer and seller that the doctrine of 'customer service' has grown up, which tries to compensate for the tendency towards separation. After all, you wouldn't need a special customer service effort if customer service came naturally or without some emotional cost.

What follows are two stories of how the divide has been radically overcome. In the first, the notion of standing in the customer's shoes became almost literally true. In the second, it was a question not of the seller going to stand on the buyer's side of the table, but getting the buyer to come and stand on the seller's side. In their different ways, both were highly effective.

*Story one.* I was running a workshop for about twenty senior managers from a retail bank who were part of a project to drive up customer service. We embarked on a classic enquiry as to what it would be like to stand in their customers' shoes. The senior managers readily acknowledged that their customers were much less well off than they were. Their incomes would be many times lower than their own, and there were plenty who were struggling with debt.

No surprises there. What my colleagues and I did was to shift the discussion away from this rational account of their customer experience to a more emotional one. We asked them what it would actually feel like to be paid much less than they were, to be struggling with debt. Before long, the language changed from a purely analytical to a more emotional one. They began talking about being in debt as 'trying to keep your head above water', 'feeling like you're drowning in debt', 'being in it up to my eyes', 'being in over my head'. Debt, it seemed, was like being in water and out of control.

So we took it to the next level. First, we got these nice senior managers to live on the average salary of their customers for a week, precisely so they could feel what it was like. We also took them to a swimming pool and got them to experience their own metaphors. We made them tread water in the deep end until they started to get that sense of not quite being in control, of being inundated with 'debt'. This meant they went from thinking about their customers to feeling what it was like to be them. As a result, they redesigned the customer service programme from the ground up, with far greater emphasis on real customer experience.

*Story two.* Let's call the company in question 'ABC'. ABC is an American advertising agency that wanted to mark itself out from other advertising agencies. Like all ad agencies it had a list of clients. At the top of the list were the four or five big clients who were worth most to them in a year, in dollar terms; the bottom end of the list featured a long tail of smaller clients who represented penny packets of revenue. All this was completely normal; standard practice in the business. It was also standard practice to keep the list a secret from the clients listed. Although you'd bid for work from a client, and bill them for it, you'd never actually tell them how much money you were hoping to make out of them in a given year.

But that's precisely what ABC did. Their main accounts director argued it would foster transparency and trust, thus building the relationship. ABC went to its clients and said, for example, 'This year we are hoping to make five million dollars from you; you sit at number three on our list.' The clients responded by thanking ABC for its openness and revealing what their advertising spend was for that year. Not only was the usual guessing game circumvented, the conversation became much more grown-up, and the relationship did indeed get closer, as the accounts director had predicted. Both sides could plan more effectively, and they worked together on how to get the most value out of the deal for both of them.

This is what happens in a market: as soon as you become a seller, you fabricate a somewhat abstract image of your buyer; as soon as you become a buyer, you fabricate an equally abstract image of the person selling. These abstract images might initially seem to be unavoidable, but as the two stories show, they are not. Putting them aside and dealing with the reality of the other party can pay dividends for all concerned.

# 18

# IS ALL YOUR NETWORKING ON EXPENSES?

Go into a restaurant at lunchtime in the business district of any major city and you will see fine fare being consumed on expenses. This phenomenon proves two things. First, networking and socialising in a business context is important. Second, it's not so important that anyone would pay for it out of their own pocket. It also proves, incidentally, that there is indeed such a thing as a free lunch.

This is how the business world turns. Networking is a cost to the enterprise but not to the individual, a cost to be bracketed broadly under 'marketing'. You take people out to lunch as a means of lubricating the relationship, and lubricating the relationship is a means to extracting more value from it. That's why 'marketing' is called marketing. You're working the market, and in a way that's every bit as intentional as selling things into it. In essence, you're buying relationships in order to sell to them; the one rule is for the cost of buying to be lower than the price you get when you sell.

In this model, the relationships sought and developed by networking are seen primarily as useful, especially when the relationship is with a potential customer or someone who can influence a potential customer. If the relationship is also pleasurable, that is an added bonus, but being pleasurable comes second to usefulness. What matters is that the relationship is perceived as a resource that can be purchased. For the price of a lunch or two, your company can buy a relationship with a customer, a relationship that then becomes an asset to you. It is an asset because it reduces the cost in time and effort of future sales to that customer; relationships make the sales process more efficient. And it's better to have lunch when it's voluntary to build the relationship, than to have to take someone out for lunch to make amends when the relationship is weak.

But another model exists, a model that I have adapted from David Maister, the marketing guru. On this alternative model, the relationship with the customer or potential customer is not seen primarily as useful, but pleasurable. Now you go to the networking event because you are interested in the people you might meet in themselves, not for what they might do for you. You take so-and-so out to lunch because you want to spend time with him or her, regardless of the business benefit that might accrue. You call them on their birthday not to prove what a valued customer they are, but because you want them to have a great day.

Does this alternative model sound naïve? Despite appearances, there are advantages as well as the obvious disadvantages, which I'll start with. If in Model A, networking is a cost, it's all the more so in Model B. Model A might be speculative, but it at least has an end in mind, in the form of a sale; whereas Model B is beyond speculation, and more like a pure risk. Model B involves investing money in a relationship with no view at all as to the return it might yield. As such, Model B is not only hard to justify as a financial cost, it's also a far more blatant opportunity cost. Why hang out with people who may never give you business when you could be hanging out with those who may well? Let alone getting on with the day job.

As it happens, this distinction between relationships-for-a-purpose and relationships-for-themselves goes back to Aristotle, and the philosopher was at pains to point out the superiority of the latter. But we don't need the ancient Greeks to appreciate what remains a modern-day phenomenon. The advantage of Model B is obviously that the relationship is more authentic. Equally, having to 'network' is to concede that the relationships created will be correspondingly inferior, which is why networking occasions can so often leave one feeling empty, and why connections made on LinkedIn, for example, can feel so thin. If business truly does come down to relationships, we shouldn't suppress what we already know, namely that relationships thrive when they're not constrained by the rules of networking. And yes, that would include paying for lunch out of one's own stash. In practical terms, it might be better to pay for somewhere cheap out of one's own money (and not have the other person see you picking up the tab) than pay for somewhere expensive on expenses.

In other words, going beyond risk and return altogether takes Model B outside the realm of work pure and simple. Once you 'network' with people for their own sake, the line between work and non-work begins to fade away. Business opportunities arise spontaneously, if unpredictably, out of positive personal relationships. What's more, the relationship survives the piece of business that gets done.

Model B also raises the issue of whether you should work for clients you don't like, or serve customers you don't respect. It implies, of course, that you shouldn't. The trouble with networking on expenses is that there might be a personal cost involved, after all. To network with someone you don't like for the sake of their business is to compromise your personal integrity. True, we can't like all of the people all of the time, and business isn't just about having warm, fuzzy feelings, but we know instinctively when we've crossed a line – when our networking smile is false, and we laugh just a little too much at the other person's joke.

Much of this will sound somewhat psychological, but there's a brute fact behind it. Namely, that networking, like junk mail and cold-calling, tends to attract only a disappointing percentage of potential customers approached. Gaining a productive relationship might be efficient in terms of the future sales process, but is highly inefficient in terms of all the other relationships not gained en route. Which is another argument for Model B.

# 19

# IS YOUR BUSINESS A SIGN OF THE TIMES?

In the 2000s, the 'noughties', I was a partner in a London management consultancy. It was in many ways a boom time for the industry. Consulting had established itself as a reputable career choice for graduates: less self-serving than banking, more lucrative than medicine, and not as demanding in terms of training as, say, the law. So there was plenty of supply. On the demand side, hiring consultants was no longer a rarity, not least because the 'consultancy' offered was expanding beyond its traditional form – of confidential counsel proffered by business sages to chief executives – into what you might call 'outsourced management capacity', whereby droves of young men and women clad in dark suits and toting laptop bags were despatched to implement IT and performance management systems in organisations far and wide.

One of the most critical factors in this expansion, at least in the UK, was the Labour government, which became a huge purchaser of consulting services, my firm included. So much did it spend, in fact, that one of the very first acts of the Conservative/Lib Dem coalition government succeeding it in May 2010 was to place an instant embargo on such profligacy. The boom time for those consultants with any significant public sector portfolio came to an abrupt end. Although I had by then left my firm in order to go independent, my erstwhile colleagues now found themselves standing on a dry riverbed that used to gush with the waters of public spending.

When we start businesses up, or take charge of ones that already exist, we tend to believe that their destiny lies in our hands. This is true but only up to a point, because there are wider forces at work, and not just of the economic variety. In the case of management consultancy in 2010, those forces were also political. More recently, it is technological and demographic shifts that seem most to count. In May 2012, for example, *Forbes* listed 'ten jobs that didn't exist ten years ago':

1. App developer
2. Market research data miner
3. Admissions consultants (who charge parents for advice on their kids' education)
4. Millennial generational expert
5. Social media manager
6. Chief listening officer (who tunes into the social media)
7. Cloud computing services
8. Elder care
9. Sustainability expert
10. User experience designer

It's not that clean a list, in that there are overlaps, and some refer to fields ('elder care') rather than specific jobs. You could also argue that 'market research data miner' and 'user experience designer' aren't so new either. Nevertheless, those themes of technology and demography stand out. These are the macro currents that will carry many companies, large and small, with their force, almost regardless of the intrinsic merits and blemishes such companies may possess.

The implication is that being a sign of the times is both good and bad. Good, because in riding that current, you will be spared some effort. Use the word 'digital' or 'neuro' in pretty much any bid or product or service these days, and you're sure to meet with an interested response. Bad, because the times are limited. It may be hard to imagine, but there will come a point when technology and demography don't enjoy the attention they do today, when tech innovation begins to plateau and the opportunities afforded by demographic change have mostly been mined. Obviously, you want to catch the wave before it peaks, and get out before it starts to fall.

But there are other ways of playing the game. The most straightforward is to choose an industry that's not so susceptible to such forces, the classic example being hairdressing: everyone will always need their hair cutting, even if during a recession they might go more infrequently or choose cheaper treatments. The less obvious way can be exemplified by Microsoft. In the late 1990s – in a time when apps had never been heard of – it was Microsoft rather than Apple that was grabbing the headlines. Although it's still a powerhouse, it's not the presence it once was. Does this mean it was a sign of the times of its own time? That its time has passed?

Maybe, except it's still in the technology industry, and that demise of technology I mentioned is still some way off. More important than the industry it's in, however, is what I would call its trading skill. Yes, Microsoft was borne along by the technology tide. But it also helped to create that tide by developing pioneering software, software based on its own resources, competences and assets. It wasn't just a case of good timing. Perhaps most critical of all, however, was the business model it imposed with respect to its (business) customers. By licensing its software so intensively, and securing terms that were so advantageous, Microsoft, or rather Windows and Internet Explorer, became the indispensable element in nearly all of the world's millions of computers. It's no accident that Microsoft fell foul of anti-trust legislation, as this trading skill always took it to the edge.

This wasn't a matter of the market offer: it was the contracts, the business conditions, the trade terms that made Microsoft excel as a business. Nor was it a matter of industry trends, of catching a wave, for such business nous is itself evergreen. What was canny about it is that because the software was new, those licensees were less experienced in rebutting the force of Microsoft's contracts. Blinded by science, so to speak, they were that much readier to sign on the dotted line. Surprise, surprise, when it comes to Apple, a similar logic applies. Its success lies as much in its aggressive trading terms as it does in the design and technology that so dazzles people into agreement. To exaggerate the point, you could claim that Microsoft and Apple are both contract and pricing specialists – not to mention tax experts – who just happen to be in the technology space. Hence a deeper lesson. Of course it's better to be in an industry when it's rising to its crest. But the more useful key to outliving the times might be something much drier: the terms on which you do business.

I'll conclude by returning to the consulting industry, because the terms on which it does business have themselves changed considerably with the changing times. Unsurprisingly, the shrinkage in the demand for consultancy put pressure on tariffs. A partner who could charge a day rate of £3,000 or more in 2009 found him- or herself having to slash that by as much as 50 per cent in order to win clients. Many more junior consultants who were let go by their employers became sole traders who, though relieved of contributing to corporate overheads, were forced to offer even more of a discount. But at the very same period, you had a few canny individuals who refused to become a sign of the times in the same way, and whose trading terms actually hardened, i.e. they *increased* their day rates to £5,000 and in some cases much, much more. How did they manage to outface the times like this? First, they had the sheer nerve. Second, they were versed in the truism that people (clients in this case) will attribute greater value to what comes with a higher price. Third, they linked themselves to a differentiating 'technology'. Just as Microsoft had its stand-out software, and Apple its stand-out products, so these brave souls would define themselves with a particular method, a framework, an approach, that served to demarcate them in a sea of other providers, and where possible they would license its use. Such technologies say that you're not like the rest, not another sign of the times, not another consultant having to work twice as hard to earn the same amount, but a guru.

So whether you're an independent consultant or the leader of a major tech business, the important thing is to identify which parts of your business are merely riding the times, and which are more robust. Put baldly, that means selling something different and selling it high.

# 20

# ARE YOU MAKING ENOUGH OF YOUR WEAKNESSES?

The authors of *Yes: 50 Secrets from the Science of Persuasion* have a chapter entitled 'Which Faults Unlock People's Vaults?'. They refer to research by the social scientist Gerd Bohner on turning positives into negatives, faults into advantages:

> In one study, Bohner created three different versions of an advertisement for a restaurant. One message featured only positive attributes. To take just one example, the advertisement touted the restaurant's cosy atmosphere. A second message mentioned those positive features in addition to some unrelated negative ones. For example, in addition to mentioning the cosy atmosphere, the advertisement stated that the restaurant couldn't offer dedicated parking. The third message described certain negative features and added some related positive ones. For instance, the ad described the restaurant as very small, but it also mentioned that it had a cosy atmosphere.

The third message was the most persuasive of the three. The negativity of the negative message (very small restaurant) was reduced by being directly linked to a positive (a cosy place to be). So much so that the small size of the restaurant itself could now be perceived as attractive.

I think there are clues in the Bohner research for how companies might play their weaknesses. Typically, companies will cover up their faults and divert the attention of their customers to their good points. As the song put it, 'You gotta accentuate the positive.' The counter-intuitive point suggested by Bohner, however, is that your weaknesses can become your strengths, and that in a crowded marketplace, it's these that can help you to assert a distinctive identity.

It's a point I was reminded of recently, while running a workshop for a client. The organisation concerned is based in New York, and specialises in supporting troubled families – troubled because they will have multiple, complex problems like drug addiction, unemployment, ill health, criminal behaviour, sexual abuse and illiteracy. Such families attract attention from public bodies not only because they are a nuisance in their local communities, but because they cost a great deal in terms of the resources they absorb, i.e. the welfare bill that the families rack up, not to mention all the hours given over by police officers, medics, social workers, therapists, lawyers, court officials, prison officers, debt counsellors, nutritionists, charity workers and faith leaders.

That list of professionals is germane. The list is long, and for many years policy advisers at national level have been calling for a more coordinated approach, so that the various interventions – from rehab to healthy eating plans to work programmes – can be aligned; and especially so that there is a named professional who has the main accountability for the family in question. For just as long, the families themselves have bemoaned the endless visits from what to them seem like a procession of undifferentiated bureaucrats who, for all their good intentions, appear only to condescend to them. The underlying model, in short, has been the inferior troubled family on one side and a squad of superior professionals on the other.

My client tried a different approach. The heart of it was to dissolve that opposition between the families and the professionals, an opposition that tended to emphasise the social inferiority of the families involved, while emphasising the credentials of those on the other side. It's true that the client organisation was still staffed with professionals from health, law enforcement, probation, psychotherapy, and so on, but they did something new. Among the most powerful 'interventions' they made was something incredibly simple, which took no expertise at all. It was to send to the families they were working with the CVs of their own staff. These CVs did not enumerate professional qualifications, however. Nor did they list the schools those professionals had attended, the prizes they'd won, the publications with their name on. Such 'strengths' were precisely what had been getting in the way; they had merely alienated the families that needed help.

Instead, these CVs featured a large photograph of the 'professional' concerned, along with photos of their own family, and a personal statement about themselves and how they spent their free time: walking the dog, partying, playing football, taking photos, cooking. They were presenting the reality of their personalities rather than their official profiles, and the result was profound. The everyday personalities were just as flawed, just as prone to sadness, mistakes, anxieties as the families who were their 'clients'. They revealed anything from their favourite films to their failed diets. But any mention of doctorates in social theory was removed. The families had assumed such in any case, so there was no need to rub it in. What they got instead was a human portrait that showed that the difference between the families and the professionals wasn't so great, after all. That the lives of the professionals had generally gone better was more a function of their social class and context than innate skill.

What I'm saying is that my client made a conscious decision to play on their weaknesses rather than their strengths – to present the whole reality, rather than a strategic selection of the positives. Subliminally they told their afflicted clients a simple thing: 'We are no better than you, just luckier.' The result was a huge increase in levels of trust, with trust being the foundation on which everything else could build. What previously would have been considered a weakness – feeling vulnerable in social situations, for example – could now be reframed as the basis for meaningful relationship. In fact, the professional qualifications had been an active deterrent. They might have impressed their peers, but all those professionals were mistrusted by the families who were the ostensible focus of their work. Far more effective was to come forward with the human weaknesses to which their clients could properly relate.

Needless to say, this organisation did not occupy a position in 'the market' like the small and cosy restaurant, but the point about being distinctively 'weak' can be carried over. To take a tiny example, I am a regular subscriber to a London listings magazine called *Le Cool*. It sends a weekly email with a few events for that week – 'le Monday', 'le Tuesday', and so on. I used to subscribe to *Time Out*, its more famous and substantial older brother. Everything that's in *Le Cool* is in *Time Out*, so you could argue that as a listings magazine, *Le Cool* is the inferior of the two. It's much 'weaker' in that it's far less comprehensive. And yet *Le Cool* is the publication I prefer. Nor am I alone: its audience and reputation are growing rapidly. Why? Because its weakness is its strength. The small selection of events implies curatorial judgement, as if you're being tipped off by the people in the know, the cultural cognoscenti. As I said in the opening chapter of this book, the critical thing is standing by who you are; in this case, not trying to emulate *Time Out* but having the courage of your own identity. If you stick with that principle, even an apparent defect can work in the market as a draw.

# 21

# WHY AREN'T YOU PREDICTABLE?

The bouillabaisse at London's Wild Honey restaurant is to die for. They serve it in four beautifully polished copper saucepans, one for the fish, one for the broth, and two miniature pans for the aioli and mayonnaise. So far, I've never been let down. The cooking is so reliable you could say it's entirely predictable.

Which is a good thing. In common parlance, however, 'predictable' has less than positive connotations. You wouldn't describe yourself as 'predictable' on a dating website, for example, or a CV. And yet predictable is only a synonym for reliable or consistent, and consistency is exactly what we consumers seek from vendors. When I visit my local dry cleaner, I don't want him to return my clothes sometimes clean and sometimes not. When I next fill up my car with petrol, I'd prefer the liquid not to come out the pump blue. Being predictable might sound uninspiring, but in lots of cases, that's all I want. Same again, please.

So predictability is reassuring. Not only that, but it helps establish the identity of the vendor, large or small, from whom you're buying. Any brand manager will tell you that a brand is a promise. You keep your promise by predictably doing the same thing again and again. If you're Apple, for example, you promise to keep making design-led, user-friendly, if pricey, products; and you deliver them. That's what we've come to expect, and we don't like our expectations being messed with.

All well and good, you might say, but how do you innovate? If your customers favour predictability, what can you do to break out of their very fixed expectations of who you are and what you have to offer? Despite their name, Apple couldn't credibly start selling fruit, could they? They are constrained by customer expectations to keep producing those Apple-ish gadgets. And yet for a long time they were considered one of the most innovative companies on the planet. So how do they square the circle? How do they manage to be both predictable and unpredictable at the same time?

It's a trick question, really. Innovation is part of Apple's core (no pun intended), an intrinsic component of their brand. You can predict that Apple will be unpredictable because they live or die by innovating technology products. They are predictably unpredictable. Most businesses are not defined by innovation like Apple are, even if from time to time they will launch new products or services. High-street banks will regularly offer new mortgage products, for example, but the organisations themselves are considered anything but innovative. That's partly because their brand relies heavily on the bank being a safe place to keep money, a place of probity and careful stewardship (at least in theory). I'm not sure anyone really wants an innovative bank as such. They might want those new products or new ways of accessing their money (online, mobile), but generally they take not the high road of innovation but the low road of predictability, i.e. wanting the bank to carry on being a boring old bank. Or, to cite a not completely different example, you don't want a high-security prison to be 'innovative', even if some of the medication administered to those within it might represent the latest advances in psychopharmacology.

So being known for innovation is one thing (Apple), while being less obviously innovative (banks, prisons) is another. In all cases, what counts most is the organisation doing the least possible to disrupt perceptions of it or to challenge people's expectations. Being predictable works.

In fact, predictability defines Apple products not only because they're predictably cool, user-friendly and expensive. We can also predict, more or less, what they're going to look like. They will be conspicuously 'modern' in the historical sense, i.e. drawing their inspiration from modernism, especially the modernist architecture of the 1920s and 1930s. That architecture, best represented by Le Corbusier, is generally minimalist, white, functional, clean and elegant. These external features that Le Corbusier applied to buildings have been routinely adapted into the main external features that Apple have applied to their products.

Were it not for the fact that Apple's brand screams 'Innovation!', these highly predictable aspects of Apple's product offer would in the end lead us to think that Apple is not that exciting after all. We might even conclude that they're not even predictably unpredictable, given the consistency. Maybe that sounds dispiriting, but it's actually something from which business leaders struggling to innovate can take heart. For even if you can't afford to spend as much as Apple on branding yourself, you can at least apply the lesson about predictability. Adopt a distinctive look for your products, or a distinctive feel for your services, and keep relentlessly at it. Customers love knowing what they're going to get.

# 22

# ARE YOU SEARCHING FOR INNOVATION WHERE YOU EXPECT TO FIND IT?

Recently I was invited to give the after-dinner speech at a corporate event for Rio Tinto, the multinational mining company. Before the dinner, I got talking to one of the company's senior engineers. He told me that in a certain part of the world you don't have to look that hard for diamonds. With a bit of scrabbling around, they can be found. And one of the reasons they can be found is that the local people haven't already snaffled them. Why not? Because these local people, who are what used to be called 'primitive', simply don't ascribe them any value. In the local economy the diamonds can't be exchanged. They're scarcely more valuable than the shells you might pick up on a beach.

The first lesson I drew from his story was that value is dependent on context. Although in the 'developed' world, diamonds are the very image of what's valuable, we shouldn't be deceived into believing their value intrinsic. Through a different lens, a girl's best friend becomes a villager's dirty pebble.

The second lesson has to do with innovation. We tend to associate innovation with the development of new products, whether those products exist in a commercial (tablet computers), military (pilotless drones) or medical (nano robots) sphere. We focus on the thing. So if you're in the sportswear business, you might seek competitive advantage by selling trainers that are lighter yet tougher, or mountaineering jackets that are warmer yet more breathable. This focus on the product forms the $x$ axis of innovation, so to speak, but it is only one axis. The $y$ axis is that of context.

Take the tablet computer example. At another after-dinner speech, I heard John Wood, the founder of a charity called Room to Read, talk about his organisation's efforts to raise literacy in Africa. Although he came from Microsoft, he kept talking about getting physical books into kids' hands, and setting up libraries. I thought all of that had been outstripped by tablet computers, so why bother? But he then made the killer point that in these places there's scarcely any electricity at all, let alone Wi-Fi connectivity. The tablet computer might be an innovation in California, but in the Congo it's an inert pane of glass with a dead battery. It reminded me of the famous cartoon of a dalek standing at the bottom of a staircase, flummoxed.

So that's how innovation can be defeated – the $x$ axis of product outsmarted by the $y$ axis of context. We're seeing this on a grand scale these days as high-street retailers are being put out of business by online shopping – Borders bookshops extinguished by Amazon, say. There's no point making your bookshops more attractive, your book selection more careful, your coffee more tasty – strengthening your $x$ axis – if the context has fundamentally shifted.

Are there corresponding examples of how you can make the $y$ axis work for you? Perhaps the most striking example comes from the history of art, and particularly the early twentieth century movement known as modernism, which I touched on in the last chapter. As the name suggests, it was about nothing if not innovation. Its most iconic work was not an oil painting of a king, a watercolour of a seascape or a bronze sculpture of a nude, but a toilet. A urinal, to be precise. Made, or rather 'found', by Marcel Duchamp, this work called 'Fountain' became a landmark in art history. Clearly, it had no intrinsic value, so its $x$ axis power was negligible. But once it was put in a gallery, the equation changed. The gallery was the context that suddenly conferred value on it. Thanks to the $y$ axis, the hitherto valueless ceramic object achieved a value – and not just shock value, but monetary value as a collector's piece.

The computer itself went through its own shift from $x$ axis to $y$ axis, but it was a long time ago. Today it's all about improving the product, but the true innovation happened when the $x$ word 'computer' was combined with the $y$ word 'personal'. Up to then – the mid 1970s – computers had been defined by being impersonal. They were huge and housed in the basements of scary institutions, where they whirred away inscrutably. Why would an individual possibly want one? Why would you want to 'compute' unless you had the pointy head of a scientist?

Clearly, business leaders can't take their attention off the $x$ axis. They need to be aware of developments in their industry in terms of the refinement of products and services. If you're a hotel, for example, you want to be looking for ways of making your offer more tailored to the guest without driving up your prices disproportionately. But are there $y$ axis ways of innovating in the hotel industry? We assume, for example, that hotels are for adults, but what about hotels for children? I don't mean family-friendly hotels, I mean hotels where kids go without their parents (yet with suitably qualified staff).

Strategy typically aims itself along the $x$ axis. It says, 'This is the sum total of the present reality, so let us make incremental advances within it, using more attractive prices, products or services.' It does not look at the $y$ axis, whereby you change the context itself. One practical tip on this is to unpick your assumptions. Say I ask you to imagine a surgeon. The chances are you imagine a man. 'Surgeon' is your $x$ axis term; man is your $y$ axis term, the context or hidden assumption. But if you remove the assumption that a surgeon is male, the $y$ axis comes into play. Now you can think of a female surgeon. Perhaps you can imagine a business set up by a group of female surgeons that charges a premium precisely because it's unique. After all, the reality is that surgeons don't have to be male. Once you start to think along this $y$ axis, you'll be looking for innovation in the right places.

# 23

# DO YOU WANT OTHERS TO FAIL?

A model of simplicity and brutality, the mission statement once adopted by Fujifilm has become the stuff of legend: 'Kill Kodak'. The fact that in January 2012 Kodak was forced to file for Chapter 11 bankruptcy might suggest that Fujifilm had achieved its mission, except that the causes of Kodak's demise weren't solely attributable to its Japanese rival; wider changes in the market were also factors.

Nevertheless, Fujifilm's aggressive focus on the competition is salutary. It bears out what Richard Rumelt preaches in his book *Good Strategy, Bad Strategy*. Rumelt argues that most strategies are little more than vague ambitions to do better. Instead they should at the very least identify the key obstacle to overcome, because this lends the strategy a sharpness it would otherwise lack. By naming Kodak as its specific nemesis, that is exactly what the Fujifilm statement does. The statement makes the strategy real rather than a matter of fantasy, and it is unflinchingly candid about the fact that the company is prepared to engage in mortal combat.

As it happens, the founder of Kodak, George Eastman, was to articulate an equally specific mission in the company's early days, namely to 'make the camera as convenient as the pencil'. But between this statement and 'Kill Kodak' lies a crucial difference. Eastman's attention on the product was surely commendable, but compared to Fujifilm's almost feral ambition, it comes across as short-sighted, because too much attention paid to the product is attention diverted away from the competition. Concentrating on the enemy might be the more effective driver of product innovation because it provides a tangible benchmark to beat. It also engages the company's visceral energies.

In fact, most mission statements, like the so-called strategies deplored by Richard Rumelt, fail to name the competition. They prefer to concentrate on what the company wishes to achieve, as if the company were in a bubble, splendidly isolated from the market. Nor is the lack of attention on the competition restricted to the mission statement. All too many companies conduct their daily business as if the market were simply the context in which they operate, rather than a properly hostile environment or one they can transform.

Take the example of supermarkets in the UK. Although there is a premium and a budget end of the market, represented by Waitrose and Lidl respectively, the dominant supermarkets, Tesco, Asda, Morrisons and Sainsbury's, operate in what you could call a 'squeezed middle'. In this space, supermarkets will actively try to woo customers by showing how much less a particular product like a shampoo will cost in their store versus a store operated by the competition. On the surface, such behaviour might look like genuine aggression à la Fujifilm. But at most it's an attempt to win some extra market share, not to put each other out of business. It's as if they simply accept the existence of other teams on the field.

At one level, of course, they are right. There are laws against monopolies. Like most capitalist countries, the UK would not tolerate a situation which led to a single incumbent in a given market. The risk of an increase in prices and a decrease in quality would be too great to bear. Undeniably that is right for the consumer, but supermarket bosses appear to have internalised this political reality at a cost. Yes, they will bear down on their suppliers, they will be ruthless about efficiencies in the business, but the intent to seriously overcome competitors appears relatively weak, and that means they're not in the business of true ambition (like Fujifilm) so much as the business of effective management, i.e. just managing the margin. And since the margins are so tight, affording little room for manoeuvre on price, the emphasis shifts towards customer service. Pleasing the customer takes precedence over killing the competition.

I'm arguing, therefore, that although customer service provides one source of competitive advantage, it ignores the other one implicit in the very word 'competitive'. Don't just focus on the customer and do what's right for them; focus on the competition and do what's wrong for them too. As Richard Rumelt is at pains to point out, it's a question of locating your competitor's Achilles heel and doing all you can to take advantage of it.

Perhaps the best-known example is represented by Dyson. If the brand dominance of Hoover has receded, it's due in no small measure to James Dyson's original insights into the weak points of the competition he was up against. As we know, Hoover was so familiar a feature in the home that the brand name Hoover became the generic name for all vacuum cleaners. As such, it seemed unassailable. But this was an illusion, because this ubiquitous product nevertheless had certain fundamental flaws. People may have got used to them because they thought that's what hoovering was, but the flaws were there: limited suction; poor reach into corners and under ledges; as well as the filthy vacuum bag and the even filthier process of changing it, let alone having to empty it out to see if you'd accidentally sucked up a precious ring. Look at a Dyson vacuum cleaner and you'll understand that its design begins very explicitly as a response to such flaws. This approach was not about making a better Hoover, i.e. taking the same template and upgrading it. No, it was a direct analysis of the weaknesses in the competitor's product. Where others fail is exactly where you might succeed.

# 24

# DO YOU EVEN KNOW
# WHAT THE MARKET IS?

I am having coffee with the managing director of an Indian digital marketing firm. The sun is beating down, and I am straining to hear him above the surrounding din. But what's clear is that he believes the description of India as an 'emerging market' represents a belated sign of colonialism. When Westerners speak about the so-called BRIC countries, they do so with as much condescension as when they talk about Africa 'maturing'.

He's probably right. Westerners tend to think that 'developing' countries simply lag behind their own advanced state of development, the latter being the obvious model to emulate. Yet as in the Arab Spring, when the West assumed the countries concerned would simply download and install a Western template of democracy, only to realise things were more complicated, there are factors in emerging markets that will cause them to 'emerge' in ways that deviate from the Western standard.

This unpredictability isn't limited to emerging markets. You can do all the strategic analysis in the world, all the scenario planning, and you'll still not safely predict the reality that will ultimately emerge. I believe it's an essential, as opposed to an anomalous, feature of the market that it contains surprises.

The implication being that (a) 'knowing what the market is' will never be completely achievable, and (b) risk and speculation play an intrinsic part.

That sounds like a problem, but it needn't be, not if you turn the telescope the other way round, and become the one who does the surprising. I'm thinking of the six-step theorem propounded by two professors at London Business School, Jules Goddard and Tony Eccles. Their logic runs as follows:

1. As competitors, we differ from each other, knowingly or tacitly, in the beliefs that drive our respective decisions and actions.
2. Because we inhabit the same reality, most of these beliefs will be shared between us and our competitors.
3. Only those beliefs that differentiate us and our competitors, including those beliefs that underpin the skills of implementation, can explain differences of performance between us.
4. Winning strategies are based on belief systems that are closer to the truth than those of losing strategies.
5. Beliefs that we and our competitors share, whether true or false, cannot be the cause of differential performance between us.
6. Strategising is therefore a discovery process, where the game is won by those who acquire sense and discard nonsense faster than their rivals.

The idea is that you want to focus on beliefs that are true but not shared – private insights, if you like. In the language I've been using, this means isolating whatever it is among your beliefs that could cause a surprise – the kind of thing that makes people exclaim, 'I wish I'd thought of that!' The

Post-it note might be a good example. People weren't clamouring for Post-its before they were invented, but once they were, those same people couldn't get enough of them. And for Post-its to be invented, there will have been some belief, held by the people behind Post-its (but not their competitors), that small, square, yellow, sticky bits of paper were just what everyone was unwittingly waiting for. What makes markets evolve are those innovations that were not predicted but were nevertheless based on a hidden truth about the market or, in other words, what customers didn't know they wanted.

I like this theorem, not least because it supports what I say elsewhere in this book about innovation having to come as much from within as without. Companies should generally avoid mimicking other companies, and go digging for resources closer to home. The theorem also suggests that there are always two types of market operating in parallel. There's the visible market, in which you can see the competition and the customers, and of which you enjoy a certain share. It's the movements in this visible market from which a strategy will try to extrapolate trends for your own enterprise to exploit. Then there's the invisible market, which strategy can't spy into, made up of competitors who are paying attention to their own private insights or 'true beliefs' about what customers might want, and developing products and services accordingly. When the visible market does evolve, it won't do so because of what could have been predicted about it by a strategy; it evolves when the invisible becomes visible and the market irreversibly changes shape. It then continues in its new visible form, acquiring some superficial predictability, until the next new product or service from the invisible market arrives as if from nowhere.

To be clear, I'm not advocating ignoring one's competitors.

The visible market needs attention, and research on the competition is essential: you need to understand exactly what it is that customers are buying and why they buy it; and you need to know where precisely the limits of the existing offer to customers lie. But the invisible market can only lie within your own organisation, or within the organisations run by your competitors. In the terms of Goddard and Eccles, it's made up of the true beliefs that no one else shares yet. It's these beliefs from which the market of the future will emerge.

# PART 3

# IN YOUR ORGANISATION

# INTRODUCTION

The very word 'organisation' contains a mixed message. On the one hand, an organisation is that which has organised things – work, people, money, desks – into a set shape. It suggests control and order. On the other hand, 'organisation' reminds us of the organic, of organs and organisms. These are entities that change and grow, whose shape is protean.

Being both of these things, structured and free flow, the 'organisation' I consider in this part is one that has to strike a balance between establishing order and going with the spirit inside. For the leader, that means knowing when to exert your authority and when to let people explore possibilities you hadn't mandated.

Not that there's an either/or. The famous framework that answers this conundrum is that of 'tight/loose'. Be very tight about the few crucial things that matter – principally the outcomes that are not negotiable; and be very loose about how people go about achieving those outcomes.

That said, there ought to be a bias towards the organic. The reality of running a business is that the organisational problems thrown at you are rarely structural. They're mainly political or tactical or emotional. I write this late at night, on the train back from a dinner with a board I consult to. The evening was billed as 'Board Strategy'. But no sooner had the chief executive given his spiel about the strategic framework and the objectives underpinning it, than the discussion turned to how to engage a workforce that is stuck in the past and likely to resist. That's what an organisation is: human energy with a life of its own.

Organisational reality is like social reality. It has its own idiosyncrasies and mores. One wants to encourage this reality not least because it helps the organisation become distinctive in the marketplace too. But one also needs to 'organise' it in some way in order to stop it becoming self-serving, to leverage it for the maximum value.

# 25

# WHY ISN'T EVERYTHING PERFECT?

I am sitting with Abraham, the operations director of a major funding body. I ask him what his strategy is. 'To make myself redundant,' he replies. Seeing my quizzical look, he explains that funding should be a completely automated process. You establish the criteria by which the organisations seeking money are judged, and they are awarded a number of points depending on how closely those criteria are met. The number of points translates into a sum of money. The money is then despatched – electronically, like the rest of the process. 'It should be possible for this business to be run by monkeys.'

Abraham's answer adds to my belief that strategies are often exercises in idealisation. For all his emphasis on the rational, he's describing a fantasy, a perfect world in which everything runs smoothly, with no need of intervention by human hand.

This isn't to invalidate everything he says. Who can argue with the proposition that the funding process can and should be automated as far as possible? It would save time, money and effort. Indeed, in his somewhat geeky way he has successfully automated large parts of his operation. But some parts refuse to be contained by his system, which is known as Green. For occasionally two organisations will tie on points. Obviously Abraham has anticipated this, so he has a weighting framework and a set of algorithms, designed to force discrimination between the two previously undifferentiated bidders. This is the second-level, more nuanced system known as Amber, in which fractions of points can be awarded, not just whole numbers. Where bidder A and bidder B were tied on 7 points out of 10, now bidder A is judged to have achieved 7.3 against bidder B's 7.1.

As you'll have guessed, it happens – if only once in a blue moon – that even in Amber, two organisations will remain tied. Both will score 7.2. What then? Then we go to system Red. Except that system Red is not a system at all. If the sum of money bid for falls below a certain threshold, Abraham will make the call himself. If it falls above, he is obliged to escalate it to the organisation's governing body for a decision. In both cases, human intervention intervenes, in the form of judgement and discretion. We're now in open country, and the decision taken can no longer be perfect. It will be arrived at through arguments as emotional as they are rational.

Perhaps that sounds like a defect, but the truth is that all genuine decisions work this way. Green and Amber weren't really making decisions, they were enacting a program, a program designed precisely to eliminate decision-making. A perfect business needs no decisions to be made. Or, to put it the other way round, true *decisions* are possible only in the face of ambiguity, and it's what makes business challenging, interesting and exciting.

Most business leaders consider decision-making an integral part of the job. And in a lot of cases their decisions are absolutely made in the context of ambiguity, when whatever system they use has failed to deliver an answer, when things aren't perfect. But not always. I can mock Abraham's geeky tendencies, but he helps me realise that we make far more decisions than we need to. The most common example is 'Reinventing the Wheel', whereby a business has established a perfectly good, if not technically perfect, system; and yet the 'decision-makers' feel like they have to start from scratch. The syndrome has a cousin in 'Not Invented Here', whereby other decision-makers mistrust any decision they've not had their own hands on. In both cases much time is wasted in rejecting what was perfectly good in the name of creating something that might not be any better. The message to business leaders, therefore, is to look for where the real ambiguities and blockages lie, and concentrate their decision-making efforts on these.

I'll give another example of the human desire to resist perfection in business. In my first few weeks as a consultant, I heard talk around the office about a client considered to be a basket case. The client printed large-circulation newspapers (when such things still existed). Every day they would have to get huge batches ready to be picked up at midnight by vans that would transport them across the country. And almost every day there was a 'cock-up'. There would be typos. Pages would be missing or misnumbered. Leaflets that were supposed to go inside the paper would be left out. The ink would run dry so that a few copies were barely legible. As a consequence, the perpetrator of that particular day's snafu would be hauled into the manager's office and given a 'bollocking'. Having glass walls, this office made the scene visible to anyone who wanted to watch, and everyone did.

So they called in the management consultants (us) for some business process redesign. This we – or at least my colleagues – dutifully did. They undertook a painstaking analysis of where in the chain things were going wrong, and they proposed solutions accordingly. They rehearsed these solutions with the team in an off-site. And then they were there on the night the new process went live, to keep things on track and make sure the learning had been embedded.

It had. The night passed without a hitch. As did the next night, and the night after. In short, everything was perfect. My colleagues submitted their invoice and retired.

But the story doesn't end there. Part of the up-front agreement with this client was that we would return after three months to review progress. It was chaos. Some poor soul was in the glass office, having a strip torn off him by the manager, all merrily observed by the staff on the print floor. Our lead consultant was embarrassed. The process he and his colleagues had designed was clearly no good, or he'd failed to transfer our knowledge in a satisfactory fashion.

When things had quietened down, he took his turn to enter the glass office, expecting a bollocking of his own. What he met with instead was a manager, his client, who seemed perfectly unruffled. Our lead consultant was offered a drink (those too were the days), and the client explained that the cock-ups and the bollockings were the main reason why people came to work.

What's the moral? Most organisational strategy is aimed at producing perfection: perfect structures, perfect communications, perfect processes. The underlying belief is that an organisation is a machine that can be tuned to a T. But as I said in the introduction to this section, organisations are both mechanical and organic, never one without the other. That is the reality, and any organisational strategy has to take both into account, even though 'strategy' by its nature will struggle to account for the errant organic quality of an organisation. Factor in human reality from the start, and not only will you not be disappointed when the organisation fails to be perfect, you'll make room for what makes business properly interesting and challenging.

# 26

# DOES YOUR ORGANISATION FACE UPWARDS, INWARDS OR OUTWARDS?

By some way my most unusual consulting assignment was with the Catholic Church of England and Wales. It came about not because I'm a Catholic (I'm not) but, as is so often the case, through word of mouth. I was asked to carry out a review of the Catholic Communications Service, a small office responsible for press releases, website materials, publications, and relationships with the media. Why the review? Because at that time, in the early 2000s, when barely a day seemed to go by without fresh allegations of sexual abuse by Catholic priests, the Church's reputation was at an all-time low. Looking at how it handled its public response was therefore seen as a matter of urgency.

Much of what I discovered during the course of the review remains too confidential to disclose, but what I think I can convey in clear conscience is what in any case is in the public domain. Apart from an annual conference of bishops, meaningful dialogue within the Church seemed a rare event. Not surprising, perhaps, if you consider that dialogue is a horizontal activity that takes place among peers, whereas by definition the Catholic Church is a vertical organisation constitutionally based, like a physical church, on looking up. Up towards God, that is. This vertical axis would always trump any horizontal dialogue; what ultimately mattered was a given bishop's relationship to the divine, not to his peers. Indeed, although the Catholic Church of England and Wales has a leading figure in the Archbishop of Westminster, and the global Roman Church in the Pope, it is understood that neither is a boss in any organisational sense. No one reports to them. They are just figureheads, because in the grand scheme of things there's only one authority to be respected, and He stands a considerable way above it all.

You don't have to be a church, incidentally, to be upwards-facing. I would describe the Civil Service in similar terms. Despite many attempts at reform, aimed to get it focusing more on the 'customer', i.e. the public, the reality is that civil servants take their marching orders from ministers, and this always forces the external gaze towards the customer upwards towards Westminster. But yes, of course, the Catholic Church is an upwards-facing organisation, naturally. The consequence, however, of looking up was that it didn't look down at what was going on under its nose.

What could be a greater contrast with the Catholic Church than a media company that produces prime-time TV programmes? Although my consulting assignment with this company lasted a mere three months, it was long enough for me to bracket it among the outwards-facing. Consider its core business: making TV programmes. You soon realise when you hang around TV executives that what really exercises them is the audience ratings. This company got all its energy, all its revenue ultimately, from its shows being looked at; and it looked at how it was looked at. It is in the business of seeking affirmation, of looking outwards. All its attention was focused on the outside world.

But as with the upwards-facingness of the Catholic Church, the TV company's outwards-facingness carried a cost. It wasn't that meaningful dialogue didn't take place within it. Rather, attention on the outside world took attention away from how the organisation itself was organised, or rather not organised. I remember asking to see an organisation chart and, to my astonishment, being told no such thing existed. Small wonder there was such confusion as to roles and responsibilities below the leader.

My last example is of an inwards-facing entity: neither a religion nor a business, but a country. Elsewhere in this book I have alluded to the economic costs of Japan's inwards-facingness. What comes to mind now is Barack Obama's chiding of David Cameron over Britain's 'changed relationship' with the European Union. Essentially, Obama warned Cameron that countries who turn inwards do so at their peril. The British right wing, by contrast, argue that the nation's identity, independence and economic strength is itself imperilled by looking towards the Continent. Cameron effectively told Obama to mind his own business. In a business context, I'm reminded of working in a consultancy where the number of internal meetings was way out of proportion. A consultancy gets its fees and its energy from working with clients. Spending too much time gazing at its own navel patently generates no revenue, and before long saps the organisation's energy too.

In all three cases – Catholic Church, TV company and Britain – we see a preferred style of operation, be it upwards, outwards or inwards. I don't believe that organisations (broadly conceived) cannot have such preferences; it's partly what defines them. But of course the key is to compensate for this bias. If you're the Catholic Church, you need to look up less and look down a bit more at what's being brushed under the carpet. If you're the TV company, look out less and pay some regard to how you've organised yourselves. If you're Britain, stop being so obsessed with Britishness (even as I write this, there's another radio programme on the subject), and reach beyond the sceptred isles. As a business leader, you'll know instinctively which bias your organisation has. The question is how soon you're going to correct it.

# 27

# WHAT'S THE ITCH?

For some years I have enjoyed a loose association with a company specialising in innovation. Innovation as opposed to creativity, that is. When for a series of podcasts on the subject, I interviewed their co-founder, he was keen to make the distinction crystal clear. Creativity is just about having interesting thoughts; innovation means turning those thoughts into ideas that work and can be sold. And so this company works on design, like coming up with innovative packaging for breakfast cereals, or developing a new brand for a petrol retailer. Much of it is pretty cool – as are their offices around the world and the people who work in them.

Alongside product innovation, this particular company helps its clients develop the skills to innovate. It seeks to build an organisation's overall innovation capability, rather than just doing it for them. On this side of the business, it more resembles a consultancy than a design house. It shows organisations how to try new things, how to experience the world differently, how to behave in ways they hadn't thought of. In short, I am describing a successful, dynamic company doing interesting things, with a team of bright, motivated and fun people. So what's the problem?

I see the co-founder or one of his colleagues no more than about three times a year. But every time I do, I hear a variation on the same phrase. The phrase is: 'We've made some changes, and now we're getting a lot clearer on where we're going.' The first few times, I took it at face value. These days, I have a different reaction. Although I still smile and nod and ask the relevant questions, what I'm thinking is that this is a company with an itch. The itch is the need to innovate on itself. And like any itch, scratching doesn't help. The relief it brings is only temporary.

The general pathology of which the scratch is a symptom is that of investing energy in affairs that don't provide much of a return. I could be wrong, but it seems to me that the fortunes of this company have depended much more on their intrinsic skills and external forces (the market) than on these structural rethinks. Restructuring is the classic way of diverting energy away from the work at hand. Ask anyone in a government body, for instance, what it's like to have your department relabelled and reshuffled every time there's a new administration. They'll tell you it wasn't worth the effort. The old way of doing things just carries on under a different name.

But restructuring is a soft target, and in any case it's not what I mean by an organisational itch. The point about this company is that they apply the expertise they have evolved for clients upon themselves. Innovation is in their blood, so small wonder they can't help becoming their own customers. Don't get me wrong: it is a wonderful company, and being innovative inside your own organisation is a fine thing, but the itch seems never to go away.

It's not just them. I think there is a broader rule. Probably the longest consulting project I have ever undertaken was with the Foreign and Commonwealth Office (FCO), an organisation with a distinctive itch of its own. Again it is to do with transferring the skills deployed in their core business into their organisation. What is that core business? Diplomacy.

What does diplomacy consist in? Talking. To use Churchill's phrase, diplomacy is 'jaw-jaw' as opposed to 'war-war'. It might sound trivial, but talking is vital because it diffuses or at least defers hostilities. As long as you're talking, there's a reduced chance of matters coming to a head. In an important sense, diplomacy is about involving people in discussion, and putting off the moment of truth. It's not just that it's good to talk, but that the consequences of not doing so can be very serious indeed.

In the world of bilateral relations and multilateral politics, jaw-jaw is all well and good. But in an organisational context, it can be frustrating, to put it mildly. The project I had a hand in involved refocusing the FCO on a set of general themes such as 'sustainable development' and 'conflict', as opposed to specific geographies like 'South East Asia' and 'MENA' (Middle East North Africa). Being the FCO, it dealt with this proposed change in the same way it dealt with potentially hazardous developments in the political sphere. It talked about it. Specifically, it emailed about it, from all the 250 or so embassies around the world in all their various time-zones. What mattered was keeping up with the debate – contributing to, influencing, shaping and above all extending it. For a consultant trying to get a handle on what the client wanted, it was disastrous. For the FCO, it was business as usual. In the end, I argued for an internal email account of my own, and joined in. I scratched away with everyone else.

I could list many other organisations I have seen who have an itch they unconsciously reach for: investment banks who literally treat their staff like assets, i.e. commodities not just to be invested in but divested, dumped at will; charities who, on the contrary, treat every staff member like a worthy cause; law firms who think of managing people as a forensic problem. It's a kind of category mistake they make, conducting themselves in the mode of their core business. Obviously, I am advocating making more of a separation between the two. The real issue isn't the time wasted scratching, it's that the organisations who are prone to it lose the ability to see themselves with any kind of perspective. The moral is to stop scratching and stand back.

# 28

# IS YOUR ORGANISATION DUMBER THAN ITS PEOPLE?

This book, *The Reality Test*, is not the first of mine to be published by Profile Books. I have two other titles with them, both works of popular philosophy. When the earlier of these, *Breakfast with Socrates*, was having its first print run, I went with my editor to observe the process live. My pleasure at watching what seemed like a never-ending stream of my own work being printed and bound was confined only by the fact that the printers were simultaneously doing Dan Brown's *The Lost Symbol*. My 7,000 copies looked like a molehill next to his mountain of 1.2 million.

Now, you can't print 7,000 books, let alone a million plus, by hand. The process needs to be automated, and so it has been since the seminal invention of the printing press. This is the first method by which an organisation can become smarter than the people within it. It might have been humans that invented the machine in the first place, but once invented, that machine allows the organisation to be many times smarter and more efficient than any effort made by human hand.

The other method involves no machine at all. Simply supplement a single human being with another human being and you have not just two individuals doing their own thing, but two individuals relating to each other and adding value to each other's work. Such is the miracle of synergy: one plus one equals three. The two individuals have organised themselves into an organisation that is smarter than either in isolation.

Except it doesn't always play out like that. There's an ancient Sufi saying, 'You think because you understand one you must understand two, because one and one makes two. But you must also understand and.' I have made the untested assumption that when you supplement one human being with another in the workplace, both share the same goal. I have assumed the 'and' is secure. Of course, as long as they do indeed share that goal, all shall be well. There's a mutual interest in supporting each other. But as we know, all too many 'organisations' are populated by factions that not only do not support each other, they actively undermine the other's efforts, causing the 'organisation' to become something less than optimally organised.

Take the infrastructure firm I did some consulting for. By 'infrastructure' I mean railways, roads and buildings. It was along these lines that the firm was organised, with a railways division, a roads division, and so on. Interviewing a range of managers from across these divisions, my colleagues and I soon uncovered a powerful ethic of internal competition. The railway guys loved it when the road guys messed up, and vice versa. This wasn't 'an' organisation but a series of tribes gathered under a single brand that projected externally a unity that internally didn't exist.

This delink in the brand between the inside and the outside world came about because the employees believed the inside was where reality began and ended. They seldom thought about the customer – the people who offered them the contracts – or the wider public, who would be using the transport they helped to build. In the jargon, there was no 'line of sight' between what the employees did on a daily basis, churning up tarmac or laying cables, and the ultimate beneficiaries of their work. And so they turned their energies to what the other guys inside the organisation were doing, where they were going wrong and how they might be thwarted further. Say they were modernising a railway station, which required train tracks, a building and an approach road for cars, the different divisions would arrive on-site and stand in their tribes, casting hostile glances and going out of their way to make the others' lives difficult. If ever there was a dumb organisation, this was it: substantially less than the sum of its parts.

Not surprisingly, our work as consultants was to help them make a link to a purpose that could unite them all. But what we found was that the tie to the tribe was stronger than to the organisation as a whole. My reflection on this is that loyalty is local. Belonging to one tribe implicitly involves withdrawing from a wider, more amorphous collection of people. The tribe is like a black dot within a blank circle, and it's the black dot that has meaning. What we needed to do as consultants was to help make the dot as big as the whole circle, and then see that whole circle as a black dot within a larger circle still. In other words, make the organisation as a whole become the tribe in relation to the market. Only then could it become smarter than its people, in the best possible way.

# 29

# DO YOU HAVE TO PLAY THE GAME TO FIT IN?

I am in Hong Kong, one in a consortium of consultants and event producers. We are in the main auditorium, doing the final run-through of the conference that will begin in the next hour, testing microphones and making last-minute corrections to the slides that will go on the large screen. Outside in the waiting area, the delegates are mingling over their morning coffee.

The conference is for the top 200 managers of a South African manufacturing company, and when the doors open to let them in, I am immediately struck by something that has little to do with the content of the conference at all. It's their clothes. Although these men – over 90 per cent of them are men – come from countries as far apart as South Africa, Poland, Israel and China, they are dressed almost identically. A pair of khaki chinos, moccasins/deck shoes, an open-neck striped or checked shirt, plus an optional blue blazer. And when the CEO hops onto the stage to deliver his keynote, his wardrobe faithfully reflects that of his audience.

Or is the audience reflecting him? Has each person privately considered what to wear in advance, and concluded it's best to dress like the boss? Hardly. The boss just isn't the kind of person to invite hero-worship, and this is no cult. Nevertheless, one might say that the clothes – the uniform, in effect

– signal a particularly strong sense of group identity, of belonging to something shared.

To me this speaks again to the limits of the strategy view of business. When people gather together to do work, it may indeed be true that the primary purpose is to pursue a particular goal – to fulfil a 'mission', as it's known. But the desire to be part of something for its own sake cannot be underestimated. Humans like to form groups – yes, around a certain purpose – but the reality, as I've suggested elsewhere, is that the belonging often becomes emotionally more compelling than the mission of the enterprise. The clothes people wear to signal their belonging is so obvious a manifestation of this urge that it's easy to miss.

The attire I describe is not unique to this company, of course. It has become a universal standard for 'business casual', marking a halfway point between suits, which for off-sites are overly formal, and jeans, which signify just a bit too much leisure. Sometimes the long sleeves are swapped for polo shirts, which creates a golfing effect and is considered acceptable because a) business generally enjoys sporting associations, and b) golf is perhaps the most corporate sport of all. But despite the universality of this look, there was at the conference so unvaried an interpretation of it that I couldn't help wondering what it takes to properly 'belong' to an organisation, and the costs of not doing so.

There is a relatively simple answer. You conform to the organisation's dress code so that you don't stand out. When it comes to the 'optional' game of corporate golf itself, you join in even if you would rather be at home with your family, because not joining in draws attention to the possibility that you don't really belong. And if you don't really belong, then regardless of your performance at work, and all other things being equal, your job will be slightly more at risk than that of someone who does. I once had a colleague who was fired because she preferred not to wear shoes in the office, to go barefoot. Naturally, that wasn't the reason given, but psychologically it was the tipping point.

People in businesses instinctively know this – they know there are rules of belonging, and that to get ahead you have to look and sound like those people who are in charge. But they equally know it's a liability. If an organisation recruits and promotes in the image of its leaders, that organisation ends up a very non-diverse place, and a lack of diversity translates into a business risk. It reduces the possibility of challenge from within, so that decisions are less robust than they would have been had they been properly tested, and can mean a narrower knowledge of the market.

Occasionally, organisations will try to compensate for the sameness of their staff by hiring someone different. This person is supposed to act as 'grit in the oyster'. One of my clients represented such grit. Thick-set, with a working-class accent, a background in manufacturing and a comprehensive school upbringing, he was recruited into a section of the blue-blooded Civil Service. Among the mandarins and the policy wonks, the Oxbridge degrees and the drafting skills, this man stood out. Or at least, he would have done, had he not been physically short, a direct manifestation of what his new colleagues took to be his general inferiority. Grit in the oyster he surely was, bringing a tough eye on the numbers and a flair for innovation. Against the Civil Service's explicit goals to modernise itself and be more business-focused and risk-taking, he was a star. Against the implicit goals, however, he was doomed to fail. 'He speaks a different language,' they said. What they meant was, 'He's not one of us.' The organisation ended up rejecting him much like an organism rejects a foreign body – a case of the 'organic' quality of the organisation dominating the organised structure and the rational attempt to fit people into it. Yes, it rejected him, even though, in his case, he was actually performing better than his peers. It seems that to some people, an oyster tastes better without the grit.

This tension between performance and belonging is, I believe, a crucial matter for business leaders when thinking about who to promote, who to give a special project to, or who to line up in the succession plan. Those leaders tend to equate belonging with trust, i.e. it's easier to trust someone if you think they're one of yours. But that's taking a rather primitive approach. The truth is that it's good performance that bolsters the right to belong, because that is what's best for the enterprise as a whole. In an extreme case, you could hire only 'belongers' and no 'performers' and the result would be a weakening of the organisation, as happens genetically in cases of inbreeding.

I am not saying it is better to perform well than to belong well, because that instinct every organisation has to spit out what it doesn't recognise as its own is probably too strong to master. What I am saying is that leaders will tend to favour belonging over performance, and that it would be better if they could strike a balance between the two. A practical way of doing that when it comes, say, to promotion, would be to do the first sift of candidates with their names removed, so that you're looking at performance data exclusively. You make a short list based on this objective method, and then you interview – with all your 'belonging' prejudices in place. Or the other way round. In either case, you're trying to get a balance between belonging and performance that will serve both the vitality of the enterprise and the comfort of those leading it.

# 30

# IS YOUR BUSINESS A HAPPY FAMILY?

They say that organisations are like families. There are the senior members who function as the elders, and the juniors who play a role akin to that of the children. Sometimes there'll be an obvious 'daddy' or 'mummy', or both. Over time, the way people in a given organisation behave with each other becomes idiosyncratic. In-jokes emerge, traditions develop, rituals repeat, and certain words or phrases take on special resonance, just like a family with its own way of doing things.

There is an innovative method of understanding families that is being increasingly adapted to the world of the organisation. It takes the metaphorical resemblance between family and organisation and pushes it into reality. I'm referring specifically to the work of Bert Hellinger. As a family therapist, he developed a set of principles according to which family systems can prosper, principles latterly translated into an organisational context.

The table opposite puts these two sets of principles in apposition. Or to be precise, it lists the family principles and from them derives questions to ask in an organisation. It's taken from an article on Hellinger by Sebastian Green, Professor of Strategic Management at University College Cork, Ireland.

| Family system principles | Organisational questions |
|---|---|
| 1. Everybody in the system needs to belong. | Who is missing: ignored, forgotten, marginalised, or excluded? Have people been dismissed unfairly? Are people who have 'energetically' left still present in the system? Do we know of and respect our predecessors and their achievements? |
| 2. Everybody needs honouring and to be in their right place. | Is the past honoured and acknowledged? Are people treated as objects or with dignity? Is length of service acknowledged? |
| 3. Those who come later take from those who came earlier. This order of precedence must be honoured. | Is the hierarchy of role and responsibility respected? Do those with privilege and power accept their responsibility to those they serve? |
| 4. There is a hierarchy between parents and children: parents give; children take. | Do the senior staff work in the service of the company and its stakeholders? |
| 5. In a relationship between parents, the giving and taking needs to be in equilibrium. | Is work/life balance equitable? Is there a balance between what people are asked to do and the rewards they receive? Is there mutual respect? |
| 6. Guilt and merit belong with whoever earned them. | Do people take responsibility for their actions and are they held accountable? Is recognition given to those people, at all levels, who go the further mile? |

Although one could dispute the purity of the process by which the questions have been distilled from the principles, and the level of equivalence between them, I find the list rich and fascinating. I'm increasingly working with such principles and questions in my own consulting practice, more or less explicitly, depending on the receptivity of the client in question.

The main emphasis of this approach is on having things in their right place, even if, on paper, the principles can appear somewhat prescriptive and notably conservative. There is a strong sense of order that lies beneath them, as if there were a universally right way to organise an organisation. Yet despite these normative aspects, it is hard to argue with the idea that people should take responsibility for their actions, say, or that a balance of give and take is a good thing. What's more, these apparently 'normative' aspects are actually designed to take account of the reality that an organisation is made up not just of the high-value employees, but everyone, junior and senior, past and present, who has made a contribution.

Out of these principles and questions, I want to dwell for a moment on just the first: 'Everybody in the system needs to belong.' According to Hellinger, when a certain member of a family gets excluded, ostracised, overlooked or forgotten, it causes a negative impact on the family as a whole. Spookily, Hellinger argues that the excluded party will be unconsciously represented by someone in the core family group, usually a child. The child identifies with the outcast, and finds itself unwittingly mimicking their behaviour. Conversely, when the family includes the black sheep, everyone thrives. The need for them to be represented unconsciously goes away, because they are accepted in their own right.

Now translate that into an organisational setting. Sebastian Green asks, 'Who is missing: ignored, forgotten, marginalised, or excluded? Have people been dismissed unfairly? Are people who have "energetically" left still present in the system? Do we know of and respect our predecessors and their achievements?' When he speaks of those 'dismissed unfairly', what will spring to mind are cases of unjust sackings that leave a bad smell in the organisation long after the event – cases where someone is scapegoated, and their departure does the opposite of healing the organisation they have left. And when he speaks of 'our predecessors and their achievements', we might remember those change initiatives which begin from a blank sheet of paper, as if everything in the past were rubbish to be thrown away; in my experience, such initiatives end up repeating previous mistakes rather than moving on from them.

The connection between a family and an organisation isn't always metaphorical, of course. In a family business, it's real. I did some pro bono consulting for a family business in South Africa that owned a great deal of commercial real estate as well as farmland, from both of which it exacted substantial rents. The paterfamilias was an alpha male with a son and two daughters. The son had a hard time competing with this domineering father, and elected to drop out. And having dropped out he was treated with all the more contempt, as if the worthlessness his father originally suspected in him had been proven. As the father got older, his two daughters took the business over, but it was never the presence it had been in its glory days. Despite plenty of work on strategy, it all felt underpowered, and the money didn't flow in the way it once had. You might be wondering whether this was the fault of the two daughters, but both were educated, savvy, personable and hard-working.

The situation deteriorated until something was said by the teenage son of one of the daughters, i.e. the grandson of the alpha male and the nephew of the black sheep. He said they should all get together for a crisis meeting and invite his wayward uncle, who by this time was practically living wild on the land. The meeting took place, and from that moment the fortunes of the family business revived. The uncle was given a director role alongside the sisters, and the nephew was relieved of his burden of having to speak in his uncle's place.

There's an underlying point to do with the difference, rather than the similarity, between families and organisations.

In a family, everyone has a right to belong. The right comes with birth, and being excluded from the family represents a violation of that right. You can't belong to an organisation in the same way because you can't be born into it, and so the right to belong never reaches the same level. Except, that is, for the founder, for without the founder there would be no business in the first place. No one belongs to an organisation with quite the same pre-eminence as the founder belongs or belonged. Founders therefore have a 'right' of their own. Nevertheless, I believe that on one condition the right to belong to an organisation can be available to those arriving after the founder, though it's obviously an earned right rather than a birth right. The condition is that the latecomer has the good of the organisation absolutely at heart. After all, an organisation cannot give birth to people who will belong to it in a way that families can give birth to people, so the organisation's options for generating the belonging to it are limited. It is on the basis of their good intentions for it that the organisation gives people the right to belong. And so your own organisation will more resemble a happy family the more of such people it has in it.

# 31

# WHICH LIES ARE ACCEPTABLE?

Like individuals, organisations tell themselves things that aren't necessarily true. Things that make them feel better. I shall never forget sitting in an office in Paris, at one of my clients' internal presentations about where the company had come from and where it was going. The company was a 1990s technology start-up, and they'd hired me for a one-off piece of advice on how to restructure themselves as they planned for future growth.

The managing director showed a slide with a bar graph. Each bar represented a year's revenue, from when the company started in 1998 to where it had got to at that point in time, which was 2008. In other words, it was the company's ten-year anniversary: the MD wanted to give an upbeat message to the troops.

Having put the graph on screen – shown overleaf – the MD began to interpret it for the benefit of those assembled. He said that the revenue profile showed the company had gone through a series of discrete phases. Phase one, in which he bracketed together the first four years, 1998–2001, he described as 'Lift-off'. Nothing to argue with there. The revenue had been raking happily upwards, from £1m to £2.5m. An auspicious start.

But how would he frame and describe the following seven revenue columns, which appeared to tell a less straightforward

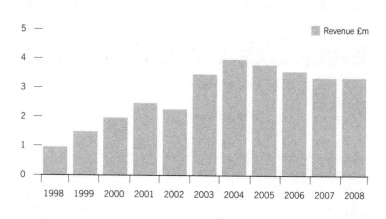

story? He selected years 2002 through 2005, labelling this phase as 'Sensing Our Potential'. The year 2004 was the tallest column on the graph, with the revenue figure reaching just under £4m, so you could see where he was coming from. The company had touched a ceiling and in the process had had an intimation of what lay on the floor above, so to speak. If you could achieve revenues of £4m, it was a sure sign that you could achieve £5m, £8m, £10m or £20m in the future. Perhaps much more.

His forcing of a phase two from the period 2002–5 logically left the last three columns to form a phase of their own. What moniker would he give to this most recent phase? The revenues in each of the three years were £3.5m, £3.3m and £3.3m respectively. He named the phase 'Platform for Growth'. His message was that, having sensed its potential, the company had consolidated, both strengthening its internal capability and codifying its intellectual property, and was therefore set for an assault on a summit that would rise high above the 2004 record. We had been pausing before the Stakh-anovist effort that lay ahead. The future would be tough, for sure, but rewarding on a level not seen before.

I sat at the back of the room, trying to mask my cynicism. Masking my cynicism about his cynicism, in effect. I saw his interpretation of the revenue figures as a cynical attempt to spin the numbers for the sake of motivating people at the end of a year in which, for the second time, a bonus would not be paid. Where he saw three discreet phases, I saw a single, starker shape: the ascent to a peak in 2004 and a subsequent decline.

That said, my interpretation also involved some glossing over of the facts. In that upwards gradient on the left of the chart, there was one year, 2002, that bucked the trend. And during the decline there were two years, the two most recent years of 2007 and 2008, in which revenues were the same. These two years could be read as plateau rather than downturn.

Which one of us was right? His optimistic or my pessimistic take on things? Neither of us was reflecting the data in a completely pure way; both of us were interpreting. If I tell you that after 2008 the company contracted further to a point in 2012 where its revenues were back down as low as £1.5m, you'll perhaps forgive me for feeling vindicated in my original interpretation. The company had peaked, the recession had hit, people had been sacked, and the few remaining souls found themselves scratching around for business in a shrinking market.

But hindsight is a wonderful thing. At the point when the presentation was made at the end of 2008, the experience of four years later was not available. Although it was my inter-pretation that was ultimately proven the correct one, I have come to believe the MD did the right thing at the time. What that thing was, in effect, was to practise an ancient philosophical doctrine called the 'noble lie'. Associated with Plato, this is a technique for use by those who have people to lead. It's OK to spin things if it helps people to understand the world around them, and if it reduces their anxiety. For when people don't understand the world around them, and their anxiety bubbles up, they're less likely to get on with the job. Uncertainty and disquiet will intrude, making it difficult for them to focus.

In that particular room in Paris on that particular day, the emotion could have gone in a number of directions. Say the graph had been projected on the screen without any commentary from the MD or anyone else. What would the team have made of it, given that there's something fundamentally ambiguous about the figures and the narrative they contain? Having no commentary at all would have done little more than generate confusion. The second option would have been to interpret the graph my way: the company's starting to fail. What would have been the result of that? Well, if there weren't such gloomy headlines about recession, people might have thought it was time to leave. Instead, they would have thought that their jobs were under threat. If the company's going down the tube, cuts will be made, and I might be a victim. A kind of concealed panic would ensue. Or there was the third option, the one adopted by the MD. With a little bit of data-massaging, he managed to soften the blow of no bonus today with a message of 'jam tomorrow'. He also gave people a story to make sense of the company's trajectory over time.

To be clear: I am not advocating the wilful misrepresentation of the facts, whereby leaders dupe their staff into thinking everything's all right when it blatantly isn't. It's more subtle than that. I'm saying that data is very often ambiguous, and that it's impossible to present it without some kind of frame or interpretation. Of course, in the rare cases where the data contains no ambiguity, it must be allowed to speak for itself. No spin allowed. But the majority of cases do require some interpreting of the facts, and this interpreting is a key function that leaders hold. It requires them to exercise discretion, to use their judgement, to make choices. After all, if everything were entirely clear, there'd be no need for leadership. The imperative for leadership starts as soon as ambiguity appears on the scene.

# 32

# WHAT DO YOU DO
# WITH THE SPIES?

My uncle, who grew up in Birmingham, found himself, once suitably qualified, in the employ of one of the city's most iconic firms, Cadburys. This was in the 1970s. The firm had been making chocolate since 1824, and although it had merged in 1969 with Schweppes, the sense of identity remained strong. What strengthened it in part was the rivalry with its great American competitor, Mars, and its eponymous bars ('A Mars a day helps you work, rest and play'). So when my uncle was recruited by this nemesis of Cadburys from across the pond, there was more than a little agitation. Upon announcing his resignation, he was marched by security guards out of the office and forbidden to return.

From the moment his Cadbury colleagues learned of his intention, my uncle was effectively viewed as a spy, as someone in possession of privileged information he might divulge to the enemy. Worse still, those colleagues will have realised that my uncle would have been in discussion with Mars for some weeks already about the job; already, therefore, acting as a potential source of leaks. In their minds, he was an unofficial traitor before he became an official one, and that made his treachery the more heinous.

From the 'secret sauce' of Coca-Cola through to Willy

Wonka's alchemical inventions, there's always been something mysterious about the essence of some super-sweet food and drink. And so, as an industry, it seems especially vulnerable to acts of espionage. But of course this is an illusion. Getting your hands on the technology for the next-generation car battery, or the formula for more effective nucleoside reverse-transcriptase inhibitors to treat AIDS, carries a value that's at least equal. Trade secrets exist in nearly every business, right down to the most banal sense that every business has its own way of doing things from which another business could learn.

One of the many differences between the 1970s and today is that our notion of loyalty to a company, and the expected length of employment in it, has changed. The 'job for life' is a thing of the past. People will now move organisations several times in a career, and may even make a switch in the career itself, i.e. not just moving from Cadburys to Mars but getting out of the chocolate industry altogether and going into journalism or IT or hotels. The risk, therefore, of employees carrying intellectual capital – if not intellectual property in the forensic sense – from one organisation to another has significantly increased.

In effect, all employees are potential spies, all holding in their heads information and insights a competitor could exploit. The question for leaders is how to deal with it. The security-guard method does little more than lock the stable door after the horse has bolted. At the other end of the spectrum, one could simply give up any hope of controlling this more or less malevolent leaking of knowledge out of one's own business: people talk, and that's that, nothing you can do about it.

There is, however, a third option. I picked up on it when, many years ago, I did some consulting for Shell, the oil giant.

Before going in, my only real impression of the company – apart from that gained from filling up my car on its forecourts – was one I had gleaned at school. It was the kind of company whose graduate training programme you would apply for. Joining Shell meant 'going into industry' but at the blue-blood, blue-chip end where all the smartest people went who didn't go into the professions. It was almost an extension of university, only with a commercial aspect. And indeed, when I was exposed to Shell in the flesh, as a consultant, these early impressions were confirmed. Yes, it was a big money company, no question, but it was a big learning company too. I was particularly aware of this because my client sat in the learning and development part of the business – not an afterthought function, as it is in many organisations, but occupying a critical place. Not least because so many of its intake had PhDs, Shell took learning very seriously.

What has this got to do with trade secrets? Shell, like Procter & Gamble or McKinsey, to name only two, is an organisation in which learning forms a key part of the offer to potential recruits. It invests significantly in it, making the employee a repository of valuable knowledge. In this there is obviously the risk I mentioned, of the employee taking that knowledge and bestowing it on another organisation later on: the spy conundrum doesn't go away. But this risk is outweighed by two key benefits.

The first I have just touched on. If you promote your company to graduates as an environment where they will learn things they can take elsewhere, it will make you all the more attractive as an employer. The 'job for life' being the anachronism it is, it's better to work with the fact than deny it. Rightly or wrongly, today's recruits have higher expectations than ever, even where the jobs are thinner on the ground.

They don't just want fair pay for a fair day's work, they want to be developed so that they can go on to the next job. Organisations might think of themselves as outlasting their employees, but the flip-side, from the employee's perspective, is that the organisation represents only a phase in a career. It offers a temporary home, like a university, to pick up new skills, new contacts, new experiences and new friends. Going with this reality and accepting that they will all be 'spies', all become transferrers of knowledge, can actually benefit the organisation. There's nothing like being viewed as a desirable employer – desirable on account of the learning you offer – because it drives up the applications and so allows you to be all the more selective in who you do take. You get the talent.

The second is the alumni effect. Again, like a university, the organisation that truly develops its people will win from them an important kind of loyalty. It's not that the developed employee won't leave, but that we become attached to the places in which we personally have made some sort of intellectual advance. There's a sense of gratitude that continues after the leaving party, after the new employment has begun, and sometimes for many years after that. This alumni network carries huge value to the organisation that did the developing originally. In the case of McKinsey, that value is brilliantly direct, in that many alumni go on to become McKinsey clients. Elsewhere the effects might be more diffuse: the alumni speaking well of their alma mater, and so gently buoying up its reputation. But such effects are no less real. These spies are less closet enemies than closet advocates.

Of course, not all intelligence gleaned within one business is transferable to another. And even where it is, technology means it may have already been shared anyway. Businesses sit in an increasingly porous knowledge network, where it's extremely hard to prevent digital flows of information across organisational boundaries, which means in turn that the value of that information decreases and businesses have to find value in other sources. But the kind of information I'm describing as being held by modern-day spies isn't of this type anyway – the trade-secret type. It's more 'This is how we used to do it at my old company': tips on ways of working, techniques for problem-solving, ideas on how to run a project, rather than factual information that can be reduced to data-bytes. In short, an organisation riddled with spies might sound like a threat, but what it really means is that you have people whose intellectual curiosity is an asset that the smart organisation will turn to its own advantage.

# 33

# HOW MUCH DEAD WOOD
# SHOULD YOU CARRY?

Cravath, Swaine & Moore LLP is an American law firm founded in 1819 and rated as one of the top legal practices in the world. Among other things, it owes its success to what has become known as an 'up or out' policy. We tend to think that such a policy refers simply to cutting out the dead wood at a given enterprise, but it's a bit more complicated than that.

According to a history of the firm quoted on a legal profession blog for law professors, the Cravath system did indeed have an 'up or out' policy, based on the belief that a 'man who is not growing professionally creates a barrier to the progress of younger men within the organization'. This belief fits with the wider Cravath ethos, as established in its early years, that a law firm should be a training ground for lawyers as much as a service for clients. Behind the ethos lay the fact that in those times, law schools were less exacting than they are today, so real-world legal practices often had to make up the difference, so to speak. Cravath seems to have taken its developmental duties towards its hires especially seriously. If after some years, certain lawyers were asked to leave, it was because their presence was a block to this ongoing flow of development from senior to junior ranks. For this firm, professional growth was key.

How different is this version of 'up or out' from those more familiar today? Now the 'up or out' policy tends to be used as a constant threat. There are companies who will annually cut adrift the bottom 10 per cent of performers – where performance is based on the money those performers earn for the company. Rather than fostering a culture of learning, it's a practice that encourages competition among individuals. And so 'up or out' becomes a matter of personal survival.

In other words, the 'up or out' policy has two strikingly different manifestations: one invites you to grow professionally; the other threatens to sack you if you don't bring home the bacon. But the difference between these manifestations is smaller than that between having a policy and not having one. Today, the adoption of 'up or out' remains more the exception than the rule. Most companies will get rid of employees only in response to circumstances, not as a matter of policy. Usually these circumstances involve a downturn in the company's fortunes, making redundancies a simple matter of necessity. Sometimes, individuals will need to be fired for very specific reasons like misconduct. Either way, you don't get rid of people until you have to. There's no standing arrangement by which the company will seek regularly to exit those people who, for one reason or another, aren't holding their own.

The consequence is what I would call corporate death row. It is populated by employees wearing invisible orange overalls. They may or may not know each other, but what they have in common is that they've been kept on by their employers in an in-between state. They no longer make a useful contribution, and yet the company won't get rid of them until a) they commit a serious offence, or b) business pressures force a wider exodus that sweeps them out the door.

Given that all organisations believe in efficiency, why

this surprising tolerance for the denizens of death row? The director of each function within the business will be able pretty quickly to identify the people who add the least value, and yet the reluctance to act in removing them can be striking. That's partly because directors don't like to offer up their own staff to be cut – it diminishes their empire, and the process is never pleasant. But it's also because, like goldfish growing to the maximum size viable in a tank, the default setting of any organisation is to expand, not contract. Just as recession is seen as a temporary setback on the inexorable march to growth, so cutting headcount in a business seems to go against the grain. Growth is the very spirit of enterprise, so being forced to cut even under-par employees can feel wrong. If nothing else, they are ballast.

All that assumes, of course, that sacking people is an option. I was once party to a conversation held by the top team of a large public sector organisation which very clearly revealed both who the 'death-row' inmates were and how keen that top team were to purge them. What stopped the hatchet from falling? The inmates were highly organised: not only did they belong to a union, they considered themselves a Trotskyite cell of resistance to management. Their underperformance had nothing to do with a lack of ability, and everything to do with a conscious political will to sabotage the organisation at any opportunity. It was only a handful of individuals, but their presence was seen as toxic. For the management to take them on would have required Thatcherite levels of determination. Inertia prevailed, the senior managers agreeing to live with this thorn in its side.

Compared with the policy practised at the august firm of Cravath, Swaine & Moore, the Trotskyite situation at the public body will seem like the opposite extreme. And indeed it is – which is instructive in that it shows that how you deal with problem staff gives a pretty accurate reading of the culture. The culture at Cravath is one of professional development – that's why certain lawyers had to be moved on. At the public sector organisation, the culture was one of accepting how things were rather than trying to change them. In other words, if you want to know what your culture is like, look at how you manage your death row.

In short, there are three types of dead wood: those who don't develop (Cravath), those who don't perform (investment banks), and those who don't do anything except undermine things from within (the public sector organisation). None of these types is particularly welcome, but in practical terms, you want to exit the saboteurs first if at all possible, the non-developers second and the underperformers last. Why get rid of the non-developers before the underperformers? Because by definition there's little chance of developing them; at least with an underperformer who's willing to develop, you can in principle make some headway.

I'll end by mentioning a fourth category that's less clear-cut. It relates to my point about organisations being not just 'organised' like a machine, but 'organic' like an organism composed of human energy. People have off days. They have off weeks. They even have off months. In performance terms, an off day equates to lost productivity, and lost productivity is what we associate with dead wood. But those same people have on days too, more on days than off days, in fact. And while they're having an on day, one of their colleagues is having an off day. There's a kind of dead-wood factor built into the rhythm of work, which affects pretty much everyone at some point. So you end up carrying someone for a bit, on the understanding that they will carry you when the time comes.

This is the fluid give-and-take that makes an organisation a social as well as a business entity, and I think it needs more emphasis than we typically give it. Why? Because it puts the overall performance of the enterprise above the performance of individuals. As long as the enterprise as a whole remains on target, it's OK for individuals to fluctuate in their performance. To be clear, I'm not speaking about those who belong to any of the three categories listed above. I'm referring to 'ordinary' workers, who perform broadly on target, but exhibit some variability. It doesn't damage the enterprise overall, and it allows for trade-offs between individuals that create a sense of social contract and mutual belonging. Most strategies are too inflexible to account for these variations, and prefer to impose a universal rule of performance rather than accept the reality of how humans operate. In doing so, they miss what is organic about an organisation, and therefore what it is that makes it a social system to which humans wish to devote their effort.

# 34

# ARE YOU THINKING TOO MUCH ABOUT YOUR CULTURE?

As I write this, I am involved in a bid for some consultancy with a German bank. Like many others in its industry, it has, in the wake of the financial crisis, come under intense social and political pressure to reform its culture. It knows it will find this hard to do without external help: culture is notoriously tricky to address from within, because you see the culture through the culture. Hence the tender.

The assumption I have made is that without such social and political pressure, the bank would have carried on as before. The question of culture would have remained unasked. Indeed, in my experience, the question of culture always goes unasked until some kind of crisis forces it. Typically, businesses will worry over the hard stuff (the numbers), and leave the soft stuff (the culture) well alone until there's a compelling reason not to. Hardly surprising, really. Any causal link between cultural change and business performance is notoriously elusive, and the soft stuff, being intangible, is difficult to get a handle on.

What's more, when organisations do finally turn to soft issues, they tend to do so in a hard way. They approach culture analytically. In the case of a bank like I am describing, this tendency may well be more pronounced. After all, they are in the numbers game. What they have indicated they want in terms of a culture-change programme is a chart with arrows on it, a list of outputs, and scorecards to show how the readiness for, or resistance to, change is dispersed across the organisation. For them, culture boils down to a mathematical problem.

From a consultant's point of view, this looks like being a tough gig. But I am emboldened by a piece of work I did with a major American media and publishing corporation. With the world becoming increasingly digital, they knew they had to adapt. This adaptation meant not just offering fewer classic products like physical books, and more services like online learning; it also meant changing the culture internally in order for it to be more alert to such opportunities in the market, and more agile in converting them. It had to shift from something old school to something much more innovative, imaginative and flexible.

Ideally, one wants the leaders to show the way in such a shift, but the truth is that most leaders are in their fifties or sixties, and their capacity to adapt will be smaller than that of their juniors. To this organisation's credit, they had identified a pool of younger, future leaders who might spearhead such a culture change, and it was with these people that I was involved. Not that this meant working with a blank sheet of paper, so to speak. Younger they may have been, but these high-potentials were still drawn from the same culture. For whatever the length of their employment, they had been looking up to those leaders for signals to follow. They might not have been set in their ways like their bosses, but the concrete was still on the way to drying. What's more, they were just as cerebral as their banker counterparts – less numerate and more literate, perhaps, but equally reliant on their brains for the solution to anything that might crop up.

The problem, therefore, was how to get these bright young things to understand their culture in a non-cerebral way. Having not thought about culture very much at all, the danger was that they would now think about it too much, and construe it in purely rational terms. Culture operates at a sub-rational level: it's what we feel when we're in an organisation, and I don't mean just emotionally. Culture also registers in the body. The clearest sense we have of it, perhaps, is when we leave one organisation to go and work at another. Ostensibly the differences between the organisations might not be so vast, but the heart and the gut pick up on what's new immediately.

Yet simply thrusting analytical people into an emotional and/or physical process is likely to generate resistance. Whatever companies say about wanting to be taken beyond their comfort zones, it's never true. Being outside the comfort zone is uncomfortable, and no client will ever thank a consultant for doing that. You have to start from where they are, build their trust and confidence, and only then lead them into the more unusual places. The task is to go comfortably into the unknown, like holding a child's hand in the dark.

To that end, we decided to work at the somatic (i.e. bodily) and emotional levels only in conjunction with the cognitive. What that meant in practice was lots of presentations and discussions on the concept of culture, alongside more left-field experiences. That way, the participants in the programme were plunged into the deep end but always had a ledge to swim back to. We got them to meditate, for example, as a way of switching off their minds, but we also gave them triangular models of the three components of culture. The three components were systems, symbols and behaviours: systems as in how things like meetings were run, how you booked rooms, how you got paid; symbols as in the company logo, individuals with big reputations, or an oft-quoted story of success; behaviours as in what people actually did, as opposed to what they thought they did.

With their rational selves given no more due than their emotional or physical selves, the participants were far more able to tune into their culture, what was good about it and what was less good about it. Or rather, what in that culture was more likely to serve the business imperative to adapt. There's no point working on culture in the abstract: it has to be in the service of strategy or it just fizzles out as irrelevant. Culture is a business lever like any other, you just have to come at it more subtly.

This is now my rule of thumb for working on culture change. Don't just work with the mind, work with the heart and the gut as well. It's these faculties that pick up the reality of the culture in a way that the mind is sometimes too sophisticated to do.

# 35

# HOW DO YOU DEAL WITH THE HIGH-PERFORMING BAD CITIZENS?

I have just come off the phone with a client – let's call him Michael – who was briefing me on the session he wants me to run next week. One of his directors – let's call him Klaus – is facing mutiny from the team of seven that report to him. While Klaus has been away on holiday, his team has gone above his head and approached Michael with a list of grievances. The list includes Klaus's inability to empower the team, his aggressive tendencies, and his failure to set out plans and objectives. The team strategy is at serious risk because of the reality of Klaus's management style. And yet among Michael's own directors – Michael is the CEO – Klaus is thought of as a star because of his professional expertise. Despite the disgruntlement he has caused among his direct reports, he is the go-to person across a whole gamut of technical matters.

To Michael, the démarche by Klaus's team comes as no surprise. He's been aware of rumblings for some time. Indeed, Michael has taken Klaus aside on more than one occasion to challenge him. Each time Klaus has accepted the criticism and vowed to do better. He's actually quite a straightforward guy, which only makes it the more perplexing. Things would be simpler, paradoxically, if he were complex. At least then Klaus could be categorised as psychologically difficult, someone not to be trusted. That would make it easier to move him on. But with Klaus, what you see is what you get.

The purpose of next week's session, therefore, is therapy. Michael doesn't use this word, but that's what it is. He says he wants a safe context facilitated by a professional (me) in which Michael, Klaus and Klaus's team can have an open conversation about what's going on. We've had strategy sessions before, but they've gone nowhere because they've failed to address the reality of the working situation. We don't need an agenda, we just need someone impartial to manage the dynamic. Things have to be aired before we can go forward.

It's by no means unusual for a client to approach me with this sort of remit. Generally I advertise myself as a board adviser, someone who can help the top team both ask and answer the most important questions about the business. But almost without fail the most important questions about the business are not business questions. Not business questions as in strategy questions, anyhow. Strategy questions like 'What size of market share can we expect in this geography?' or 'Should we shut down that product line?' don't require so much discussion, because the answers can generally be found through a bit of analysis. It's not these questions that boards and senior management teams struggle with. For example, I have the board of a large public healthcare organisation as a client, whose most vexing issue is the degree to which its values may be compromised by having to adapt to newly marketised conditions. This is a debate about ideology, and it's a lot less tractable than agreeing what share of that new market they might be able to snatch. In Michael's case the question is: 'How do you deal with the high-performing bad citizens?' His answer is next week's session.

I shall describe a comparable situation. It concerns two high performers, Mary and Pedro, who are 'bad' only in the company of each other. Both are directors of a sizable American food enterprise. The CEO uses me to run top team away-days, which typically occur twice a year. These are opportunities for the senior guys to step back, away from the hurly-burly, and grapple with some of those larger questions. At the last but one of these away-days, the discussion turned to cost-cutting. The CEO had charged each of the directors to come to the event with a plan for making savings in their division.

Mary, the operations director, volunteered to go first. The fact that she went first says something about her can-do personality. She circulated a spreadsheet identifying both headcount reduction and potential savings from process efficiencies. It amounted to 10 per cent of her budget, this being the target figure the CEO had set. Despite the cut, she was clearly pleased with herself for having performed the task in such a model fashion, like a teacher's pet. And indeed she was a star in the organisation, a young woman who had risen rapidly to this very senior role.

Last to go was the CFO, Pedro. An older, eloquent man of huge experience, he was effectively Mary's opposite. He had no figures to pass round, and intimated that the finance division wasn't really subject to the same target. He would do his best to look for savings, but warned it would be 'very difficult'. He added that cutting expertise in finance during an efficiency programme was to risk adequate supervision of that programme. The CEO nodded in understanding, and the discussion was about to pass into its next phase when Mary remonstrated. 'I can't believe it!' she said. 'How does he get off so lightly?' The colour was rising in her neck. 'Surely if you're cost-cutting, the back office is where you start! Finance should be *more* than 10 per cent, not less!' By now tears were in her eyes.

Pedro looked at her implacably, but it was obvious that just as much emotion was seething inside him. 'If you had more experience, Mary, you'd understand that good finances are not just the "back office", as you put it, but the bedrock of this organisation.' From there, the row got worse. Mary stormed out.

The following week, back in the office, when the storm had passed, the CEO asked me to mediate in a series of meetings between Mary and Pedro. Essentially, I was picking up the pieces from a cost-cutting strategy that had been devised without considering the reality of the personalities tasked with delivering it – a sadly common characteristic of strategy-making. It would have been better in any case if the CEO had thought more carefully about whether a blanket 10 per cent cut was genuinely best for the business. It looked egalitarian, for sure, but it also looked crude, and the question of whether to take more out of the front or back office should have been informed by more nuanced data. If there was so much emotion in the room the week before, it was probably because there were some real underlying issues, to do not just with the personalities but with the business operations.

In the process of the mediation meetings I learned to appreciate the difference between attitude and behaviour. The attitude held by each of the two protagonists was never going to change. Mary believed Pedro was being unjustly sheltered by the CEO, and that her customer-facing, value-creating function was unarguably more important than finance. For his part, Pedro never shifted from the attitude that his division made everything else possible, and his contempt for, or perhaps jealousy of, this female high-flyer would never dissolve. But what I could get them both to agree on was the behaviour that they would adopt in each other's company. They drew up a list of ground rules, and stuck to them.

The list was effective for three reasons. First, because in naming behaviours it gave an indication of something that could actually be done: both parties could now focus on how to be in front of the other person rather than bottling up their disdain. Second, talking about 'behaviours' took the element of blame away, because a behaviour is not an essential part of someone's character but a mode of acting in the moment. In other words, behaviour is a choice, and giving these two people the choice enabled them to feel freer and more in control of the situation. Third, the very act of drawing up ground rules gave the two parties a real and felt experience of agreeing with each other, which broke open the path, so to speak, for them to be able to agree with each other in future rather than digging into their hostile positions. The result was that these two high performers behaved like good citizens, and kept their bad-citizen selves under wraps.

# 36

# WHICH CARD WOULD CAUSE THE HOUSE TO FALL?

Recently I had the privilege of meeting a man in Tokyo who sits as a non-exec on the board of several major Japanese companies. He was addressing the subject of succession planning, except he didn't call it succession planning. He called it the most important decision a Japanese CEO thinks he can make. I can roughly transcribe his words as follows:

> The most important decision for a Japanese CEO is the appointment of his successor. In nearly every case, that successor will be like him. He will be Japanese – anything else would be inconceivable – and have joined the company straight out of university. Those who come on board even a couple of years after graduation will not be considered serious candidates. It's from the cohort of insiders that the recruitment will be made. And once the recruitment is done, the departing CEO doesn't in fact depart but takes up the position of Chairman of the Board.

The strengths and weaknesses of such a system aren't hard to list. It fosters loyalty, it preserves the corporate memory, it strengthens the internal brand, it provides stability, it builds trust, and it leverages the value to be got from long years of experience in the same company. On the other hand, it creates a clique, it promotes inwardness, it can lead to sycophancy, it could stifle innovation, and there's an increased chance of the mistakes of the past being repeated.

The Western system usually works the other way round. The CEO will often be appointed from outside the business altogether. People want a fresh pair of eyes, new blood and some wider experience – perhaps even the direct knowledge brought from a competitor. Besides, internal promotions to CEO can be tricky. Directors don't always take kindly to reporting to a former peer, especially if any of them applied for the job unsuccessfully.

But the most fundamental difference between the two systems is that in Japan you really know what you're getting, and in the West you don't. Obtain as many references, formal and informal, as you like, do as many interviews, you never really know how the new Western CEO is going to work out until he or she's got their feet under the table. Again, it's reality that trumps strategy – recruitment strategy in this case.

One of the consequences of this Western approach is that our expectations of him/her will be higher. Having less direct experience of the individual to temper those expectations means there's more opportunity for fantasy, for idealising the appointee as a hero or heroine whose touch will turn all into gold. Like football fans anticipating the arrival of a new manager from overseas, we pin our hopes on someone who can transform the fortunes of our enterprise. The vast literature on leadership only adds to the expectations, because it advances the idea that leadership is the single most critical factor in an organisation's performance. And so we come to believe in the notion of the person on whom nearly everything depends: the card that keeps the house together.

I'm not saying that leaders can't have a disproportionate effect on the entities they lead. I am currently working, for example, with the new CEO of an organisation I've consulted to over many years. That in itself is quite unusual: a new CEO will typically want his own consultants, if any, as it signals a break from the past. But now I'm working with him, just as I worked with his predecessor, it's allowed me to have a very direct sense of the difference that a single leader can make. I've discovered a number of interesting things.

The first is that the old CEO, who during his stint was highly regarded, is now spoken of in more captious terms: 'Bruce [not his real name] never had a proper grip,' or 'You always felt Bruce was too focused on winning the battle, but he was losing the war.' Correspondingly, people cite Adam [not his real name either] as being 'a breath of fresh air', 'someone with real strategic focus'. And it's true that both Board and senior management team meetings (which I'm often at) move along at a brisker pace, even while tackling the harder questions that Adam likes to pose. Like many new CEOs, Adam has also announced a restructure.

On one level, then, Adam, who has come from a business outside the sector, is having a significant impact on the organisation. But at another level, he's not, and nor is he likely to. Lower down than the Board and SMT, things feel like business as usual. And at the most junior levels, it's a bit like swimming with the deep-water fishes and being aware of activity on a boat miles above, but there being no connection between the two. In fact, most organisations are made up more of this huge body of seawater than the boat on the surface, and most CEOs never really take a swim through it. The exception being Bruce, ironically, who was a man of the people, and spent much of his time with less senior staff, building trust and commitment from them. Even though the organisation is now psychologi-cally purging itself of him to make way for the new CEO, for many years it was loyal to Bruce and did his bidding.

So what's the lesson? Adam is trying to work on the system, whereas Bruce worked with it. Adam is going for a step change that will probably end in some disappointment, given the amount of resistance he's already provoking, whereas Bruce had lower ambitions that were often satisfied. Not that these are the only alternatives, and Bruce should have done more with the support he created. The point, neverthe-less, is that a leader can indeed have a profound influence on the business, but that to go for transformation, as Adam is, you might have to do less leading, in the sense of declaring strategic intent, and more standing in the midst of the thing you want to transform. I'm not talking about 'leading from the middle': Bruce needed to be liked too much, and this meant he lost some of the detachment needed to be in charge. I'm saying that you can't lead a business through strategy alone.

You will have noticed that, being of the system rather than working on it from the top, Bruce was also a little more Japanese in his style. With the crucial proviso that he had no say in Adam's appointment.

**PART 4**

# IN YOUR HEAD

# INTRODUCTION

You've made it. You're the leader. You have people reporting to you and the biggest pay packet is yours. In meetings at the office, when you speak, your staff fall silent. When the press or shareholders or key clients ask to deal with your organisation, it's you they really want. On your CV you can put CEO. You're the big cheese.

That's the objective view. The subjective reality will be different. The chances are that you have worries. The chances are that you're not always as confident as people think you might be. The chances are that being a leader isn't as smooth and glorious as it's made out. In short, you have your demons.

The point of this part is to name those demons and try to chase them away. No doubt in your time you've been on leadership courses, and/or you've had media training and/or you've been taken through compliance issues by your head of legal and/or you've been groomed for the role and/or you've been coached. In theory, you're all set. But the reality of being a leader is never quite addressed by all of these worthy services.

Being a leader demands that you address your own personality as a key factor in the success of the enterprise that is yours to steward. This is because, at this level, your personality is not a gratuitous detail: it's the very thing that sets the tone of the business. How you relate to yourself, how comfortable you are in your own skin, will influence everything else. It might sound like psychology, but at this level, that's what business is. Who you are impacts how well your business performs.

# 37

# HOW MUCH MORE VALUABLE THAN YOUR STAFF ARE YOU?

Periodically, the question of boardroom pay comes to the fore. Hardly surprising, as the trend for executive compensation to increase appears unstoppable. In the 1970s the working ratio of the pay of the boss to that of the person on the front line was very approximately 10:1. So if the former earned $100K a year, the latter would earn $10K. Today the working ratio is closer to 75:1, and in many cases much higher. In the insurance industry, for instance, you might expect someone in a foreign call centre to earn $20K, while the most senior person might look forward to $20m in gross compensation. The ratio in that case is a staggering 1,000:1.

The defence typically offered in favour of such levels of reward is that the war for talent is global, so if you want the best CEO, you have to compete across the world, a situation which presses the figures northwards. This argument produces the image of an elite cadre of extraordinary candidates who circulate in an atmosphere of their own, several miles above everyone else. It's an image that can be hard to square, however, with the reality available to anyone with Internet access. Look at the profiles of the world's best-paid executives, and you'll find they appear not just ordinary, but nearly all of a type: white, male, heterosexual, somewhat overweight, grey or thinning hair, spectacles, suit and tie.

So the question is what makes these men somewhere between seventy-five and a thousand times more valuable than the most junior people they employ, the vast majority of whom will be socially and economically less well provided for, and so, at least on paper, far more deserving of the money going to the boss?

There's a supercilious answer to this which says you're worth whatever the market is willing to pay, but that's not very satisfactory. Essentially, we are dealing with two scales. The first is a vertical scale which distributes salaries within a single organisation; it's this scale that produces the startling ratios. The second is a horizontal scale which distributes salaries among senior people across several organisations that are considered comparable. On this second scale, the ratios almost disappear, because if you're earning $20m and the next CEO is earning $21m, the ratio barely registers.

Except, of course, that if you yourself sit on the horizontal scale, you actually experience it as vertical. The fact that you are on $20m and the next guy is on $21m becomes painful because you see him as higher up. The psychological point being that when it comes to making comparisons, we take much more account of our peers than we do of our juniors.

The trouble with this psychological preference for peer-to-peer comparison is that it allows senior executives to avoid the more testing question that forms the title of this chapter: 'How much more valuable than your staff are you?' This is not a question of how you rate against your peers; it's a more direct way of asking you as a leader to account for the value you add. Do you really add ten or seventy-five or even a thousand times more value than the most junior person in your operation? And, if your answer is yes, how do you break it down?

Methodologically, we should allow for the fact that in a given organisation, people at the top are always going to be paid more than those at the bottom, so a ratio will always apply. Coupled with this fact is the reality that a person at tier 4 today may well rise to tier 1 in a few years' time, making today's salary just a snapshot in time that shows how appropriate the salary is for now. But still, the question remains as to what exactly it is that defines the extra value you add as the person at the top. One experiment would be to take the leader away and see what difference it makes to the performance of the business. Another would be to reverse it. Send the staff away and ask the leader to do it all. He or she would very soon realise the value that other people add and start hiring them back, which should throw his or her own remuneration into pretty sharp relief.

I am attracted, if not entirely persuaded, by Elliott Jaques's stance on this question. He argues – and I paraphrase – that what sets the person at the top apart is their cognitive ability to deal with complexity. In ordinary English, that means the brainier you are, the more senior you should be and the more you should be paid. The value you add lies in being able to compute a wider range of factors than anyone else: strategic opportunity, financial risk, legal and political considerations, capacity to deliver and potential to improve efficiency, for example. I say 'compute' because it does sound a bit like being a super-computer. To push Jaques's point to an extreme, you could say that if business were a game of chess, you'd want Deep Blue running the game for you. Throw the most wicked combination of problems at it, and it will do a million calculations in a short space of time to work out the optimal course of action. For a capability like that, you might well be willing to pay $21m and rising.

It's this logic that lies behind the yearly milk round, with the corporate behemoths visiting the elite universities to attract the smartest students. It would be interesting to go back several years later and do IQ tests on those who've made it to CEO. I don't think many CEOs would be found to be the smartest person in their organisation, let alone seventy-five times smarter than the juniors. That's one reason why I'm not entirely persuaded by Jaques: the fact that no business will ever actually appoint a CEO on the sole basis of computational brainpower, even if it should. Another reason is that someone who's all brain will lack the emotional intelligence necessary to keep staff feeling motivated. Obviously enough, a leader needs both analytical and interpersonal skills, and there's value in having a good balance of the two. Such people are rare, of course, and they say that of the two, analytical skills are the easier to learn – though I once had a particularly analytically minded client who forced himself systematically to acquire as many interpersonal skills as he could, as if he were cramming for an exam.

A more distinctive way of estimating how much more valuable than your staff you are comes down to the degree to which you are personally invested – emotionally rather than financially – in the enterprise's prosperity. The more you care, the more disposed you are to do whatever's right to help the organisation flourish. You are 'more valuable' not in a technical sense, not according to a 'competence', but because you have the organisation's interests absolutely at heart. Too many of today's bosses are professional CEOs who move from one organisation to another without becoming meaningfully invested in any. The psychological effect of knowing you'll be around for a maximum of five years is that you'll care only so much. The same phenomenon is just as true at more junior levels, of course. Many front-line staff do not have the interests of the organisation at heart, seeing it as simply a vehicle for getting paid. By no means am I suggesting that caring about a business can substitute for sound leadership. Caring doesn't equate to competence, but it offers another useful, if unscientific, measure of worth.

My final point, however, stems from my experience just yesterday of sitting on the panel to appoint a chief operating officer to a professional-services organisation that is one of my clients. We interviewed the shortlist of three candidates, and easily agreed to rule out one. That left us with two, both of whom were more than competent to do the job. One had been an army officer, the other the chief executive of a law firm: totally different propositions. Initially I wondered if the army officer wouldn't be the better choice, precisely because his background would sit at an angle to the recruiting organisation, perhaps producing a creative tension. But we appointed the law-firm candidate because his background in running a successful legal practice meant he knew how to get the most out of people through means of persuasion rather than giving orders, which was much more appropriate for the staff. In terms of value, that counted pretty high, because it promised leveraging the value of the business as a whole. In other words, you're at your most valuable as a leader when you can release the maximum value from everyone else; your own value resides not in you per se but in your ability to unlock the value that resides in others.

# 38

# WHOSE LOVE DO YOU NEED?

One of my most interesting clients in the recent past was the chief executive of a Swiss pharmaceutical company. My brief was to work with the top team on the future direction of the business, though this isn't the real reason he hired me. He wanted my love.

Let me explain. He had only recently taken up his post, and the truth was that it was a big step up from the organisation he had run until that point, a mid-size R&D company based out of Geneva. A chemist by background, he had thrived in the R&D environment, enjoying the professional respect of his peers, and finding the running of the business easily within his comfort zone. The new job was a different kettle of fish. The organisation was big and sprawling, and his professional expertise as a scientist would only get him so far in leadership terms. He instantly recognised that getting the future direction clear was an essential first step – hence the assignment for which he hired me – but our conversations routinely shifted on to another topic.

'How do I compare in your experience of other chief execs?' he would ask me. 'Would you have made the same changes to the top team that I have? What's struck you about the way I communicate?'

These and other questions he would put to me, all of which were fine and normal, except that what he was really asking for was my approval. He wanted to be reassured because he was out of his depth.

Now, it's not unusual for clients to hire consultants as a kind of insurance. If the consultant says it's OK, it's probably OK; after all, they've seen lots of other organisations, so they should know. Being approved of by your consultant can seem like a good thing. You just have to set aside the fact that consultants are paid by their clients, which makes those consultants more likely to err towards the approval the client wants rather than the criticism the client sometimes needs.

I have another client who's much less needy of my love, but desperately wants the love of the city analysts who have such an influence over his company's share price. And I have a third who likes nothing more than giving speeches to large cadres of his employees and taking the applause.

Whether it's a consultant, an analyst or the staff, there's no leader, in my experience, who's not after the love of someone. It's a profoundly motivating factor. There's another chapter in this book, chapter nine, about loving money, but of course the love of money is often a stand-in for something else. For example, you love money because becoming rich is a sign of your worth in the eyes of your father. Not that the need for love in business is a bad thing. On the contrary. Being a motivating factor means it's a source of energy. There is, however, a question of balance. Loving your consultant more than your customer is a problem, just as loving your city analyst more than your staff is a problem too. These loves might be motivators in the sense that they are psychological levers that get you going, but they have to be balanced against the real-world needs of all your stakeholders. As in a romantic relationship, love can blind you to reality.

I'll illustrate the point with an example. I have French

friends who run a homeopathy business. They are a husband-and-wife team. And although any business run by a married couple will have its own share of bear-traps, the principal source of concern lies elsewhere. Originally, the business belonged to the wife's father. He, like many of his generation in the 1960s, became passionate about natural remedies, deploring the rise of 'big pharma' as represented by the client I mentioned at the beginning of this chapter. He wanted to offer more holistic solutions to the needs of patients, and established a practice in the south of France that was renowned for the dedication it showed them.

When he died, he left the business in his will to his daughter, my friend. She took on the business with a daughterly reverence for her father's original ambitions. She wished to do right by him and the legacy of which she became custodian. And so she recruited her husband into the business, conscripting him into this act of loyalty to the memory of the father she loved. Together they would keep the flame alive.

Unfortunately, the flame soon sputtered and threatened to give out. Customers stopped coming, and the business started to fail. At first, the daughter told herself she was no substitute for her father. If customers were staying away it was because they were used to him, Monsieur, the patriarch. Naturally, it would take time for them to become accustomed to the nouveau regime. Two years later, however, things had barely picked up. She felt just as ardent about keeping her father's ambitions alive, but the customers seemed even more lacklustre about the enterprise. Despite the extra capital the father had bequeathed in his will, the business found itself teetering towards bankruptcy.

The problem was that she saw the business as a means of loving her father after his death. A problem because not only did it keep her trapped in the past, it stopped her from focusing on those who were the real source of the company's future: its customers. They were the present reality, and it was this reality that was calling for the attention. After all, it was the customers that the father had been so concerned about, not the business per se. The daughter's love for him blinded her to his love for them.

Hence my point about balance. We're all in business, probably, to satisfy some psychological love. The important thing is to identify what it is, and then to realise how disproportionate is the amount of your effort it is taking up. Unfortunately, running a business really does involve trying to please all of the people all of the time, not just those whose love you seek.

# 39

# WOULD YOU GO DOWN
# WITH YOUR SHIP?

If you look up the name Mark Haysom, you will discover that in 2009 he resigned as chief executive of the Learning and Skills Council – an organisation I consulted to intermittently from its inception in 2001 until about 2006. To understand why he resigned, you have to understand two things: the business and the man.

The Learning and Skills Council, subsequently rebranded the Skills Funding Agency, was an arm's-length government body whose role it was to allocate more than £10bn of public money to Further Education colleges across England. The allocation was for colleges not just to run courses, but to maintain their facilities, and to build new buildings as appropriate. During 2009 it transpired that the LSC had promised several million pounds to various colleges to fund such capital projects, only to uncover a big hole in its accounts. The money wasn't there. The Public Accounts Committee spoke of 'catastrophic mismanagement'. Colleges who had planned courses based on the new builds, and recruited students accordingly, were caught short. The story made the front pages.

It was in the light of this debacle that Mark Haysom resigned. The word on the street was that it wasn't his fault, but as the organisation's figurehead he did the decent thing: he went down with his ship (the LSC was wound up shortly afterwards). Perhaps that's not surprising: chief executives are supposed to carry the can, and political pressure will almost certainly have been exerted. Nevertheless, his gesture of resignation suggested he was a man of principle.

There was a time when taking responsibility in this way was the norm, but in the past decade or two, things have shifted. Leaders these days tend to be a bit more defiant. Even if they do resign, they might do so without accepting the blame, the two most (in)famous UK examples being Fred Goodwin and Bob Diamond. The former heads of Royal Bank of Scotland and Barclays respectively, Goodwin and Diamond both left under a cloud of malpractice that had been alleged in their organisations, while seeking to distance themselves from it. In a letter dated 28 June 2012, to the Chair of the Treasury Select Committee, Diamond wrote:

> Barclays traders attempted to influence the bank's submissions in order to try to benefit their own desks' trading position. This is, of course, wholly inappropriate behaviour … This inappropriate conduct was limited to a small number of people.

Diamond's words make it clear that the misdemeanours at Barclays had been the fault of persons other than him. Ostensibly, he's trying to sound philosophical and contrite, but subliminally he's letting us know that he's above it all, distancing himself from the reality of his implication in it. In the same month, June 2012, some years after Goodwin's departure, the *Daily Telegraph* was reporting that:

> Former directors of Royal Bank of Scotland, including the
> lender's disgraced chief executive Fred Goodwin, have denied
> claims they did anything wrong before the bank's collapse.

Astonishing, considering that the breakdown of RBS was the largest and most spectacular in the UK's history. Besides, if they weren't responsible, they were incompetent, as they should have taken responsibility as part of their job spec.

I have placed Haysom at one end of a spectrum and Goodwin/Diamond at the other, though it would be an exaggeration to say we are talking about saints versus sinners. What we can say, however, is that such examples raise the question of how much responsibility leaders should take for the organisations they lead.

There is a potential answer in the form of RACI charting, one of the first techniques I learned as a consultant. The four capital letters stand for responsible, accountable, consulted, informed. It's a way of working out roles and responsibilities. Say I'm throwing a surprise birthday party for a friend, the RACI chart might look as follows:

| Who's responsible | Who's accountable | Who's to be consulted | Who's to be informed |
|---|---|---|---|
| I've got caterers doing the food and a DJ doing the music. They're responsible for that. | I am. If the party's a flop, it's down to me. If it's a hit, I'll take the praise. | I'm getting ideas from my friend's friends, plus I need to pick a date that most people can make. | I have to tell the neighbours as it could get loud and go on quite late. |

What's most relevant about the chart is the distinction it makes between accountability and responsibility. I'm accountable for the overall party, even if I've farmed out specific

responsibilities to other people. The Bob Diamond version of
this distinction would read as follows:

| Who's responsible | Who's accountable |
| --- | --- |
| A small number of Barclays traders. | A small number of Barclays traders (not me). |

The flaw in this Diamond is not only the blurring of the
distinction between accountability and responsibility, it's that
if all the people responsible for the bank's activities are also
accountable for them, there's no role for a chief executive. The
accountability already exists within the organisation, so the
chief executive adds nothing. He's accountable only in the
technical sense that it's him who's giving the account – the
account of his non-accountability. If he does have a role, it
seems it is to preserve his own innocence.

So there you have it: leaders are leaders only insofar as they
are prepared to take the blame as well as the praise, to be the
mirror for all the reality within their organisation. Yet along
the spectrum I have described, there is also a middle ground,
identified by the phrase 'systemic failure' or sometimes 'institutional failure'. The phrase indicates that it's hard to nail
accountability to any named persons, yet the organisation as
a whole remains undeniably culpable. So when in the wake
of the Stephen Lawrence murder in London the Metropolitan Police were found to be 'institutionally racist', it wasn't
necessarily that every officer hated ethnic minorities, but that
the culture of racism was rampant. Does that make the chief
constable accountable?

Or consider the dramatic narrative told by Scott Snook,
in his book *Friendly Fire*. The subtitle is 'The Accidental
Shootdown of US Black Hawks over Northern Iraq', and the

book relays in excruciating detail how collective disaster can result even if everyone individually is doing their job. In the Snook case, it came down to some basic things, like the fact that US aeroplanes were known as 'birds', and that because helicopters weren't also known as 'birds', the number of birds counted in the sky was smaller than the number of aircraft, which led to the excess aircraft being shot down as unidentified and therefore hostile. A tragedy, but whose fault was it?

Again, you could argue that the leader should be held to account anyway. In a sense, that's exactly what accountability is: being prepared to be held to account for things over which you had no direct control. Which implies that the true task of the leader is to set the overall tone, principles and conditions – the framework within which members of staff will take decisions when the leader's not there to oversee them. If that overall tone, as in the cases of Goodwin and Diamond, is swashbuckling, small wonder it plays out in organisational activity that sails too close to the legal wind. If on the other hand the overall tone is one of accepting the reality of financial rules and regulations, the chances are that people will follow suit. Needless to say, this second option is the one to choose if you don't wish to be pursued by the demons I mentioned in the introduction to this section.

# 40

# SHOULDN'T YOU BE PARANOID?

The Queen believes the world smells of fresh paint. So goes the saying, and it contains a discomfiting message for leaders of businesses as well as kingdoms: you're being duped.

Often the problem starts with the employee survey. Leaders are warned that they're not sufficiently 'visible' in their organisation. Dutifully enough, they take a vow to walk the floor more often, to show an interest in Marco's skiing trip or Maria's house move, to leave the office door open or to host a monthly brown-bag lunch. No doubt such efforts nudge the visibility ratings northwards, but in so doing they give the leader in question a distorted view of life on the company's inside, cosseting them from the reality.

When that leader repairs to the safety of the executive suite, the distortion resolves only so far. The colleagues might be more senior, but as long as the leader remains their leader, there'll be a tendency among them to garland the truth, a tendency that owes not least to the competitiveness that stirs among directors when gathered before the boss. Whatever their motive, the result is the same: a flattering distortion. To be a leader means, among other things, to be more or less benignly deceived.

Given this bias towards evasion and flattery on the part of their juniors, shouldn't leaders be paranoid about what's going on? About the reality that lies behind the deception? And if so, what can they do about it?

The answer is surely to foster a culture of openness, a culture where the minions feel comfortable letting the emperor know about his absence of clothing. It's particularly important in strategy season, when people tend not to point out holes in the strategy because the strategy gets seen as the incarnation of the boss's will. To challenge the strategy is to challenge his or her authority. And the lack of challenge in agreeing strategy is exactly what makes strategy weaker than reality.

Hence that need for a culture of openness. Not that it happens just like that, of course. Such a culture of openness and challenge can come about, they say, only if the leader owns up to his own mistakes first. He or she has to model such openness and so let it be shown that for those who follow suit, no thumbscrews will be brought out.

That's the textbook answer, at any rate. In my experience it doesn't always work. There's a reason people are reluctant to challenge. You cannot get round the fact that between the boss and everyone else lies a chasm. The difference between the two sides of the chasm is the level of risk involved in confessing one's sins. No matter how open the culture, the boss is the boss by virtue of the fact that he or she ultimately holds the fate of others in their hands. This right over an employee's destiny can be exercised at any time. The point being that so long as the boss has a gun you should never be the messenger, even if the gun's been put away in the drawer.

There is another approach. Or rather, the same approach implemented in a more effective way. A director of a consultancy firm once apprised me of what he called 'the obligation to dissent'. This was the code of practice espoused at the firm to ensure that everyone from novice to silverback spoke up about their concerns. You were obliged to surface doubts, problems and issues that you might otherwise hope would go away. If you didn't, you weren't doing your job.

The lesson for leaders is this: don't just encourage an open culture, don't just model it. That's not enough. You've got to demand it. A little bit of fascism to produce a bigger bit of communism, as it were. Leaders, like scientists, should be gathering all the info that doesn't fit with the existing theory or the accepted narrative, so that the truer, more inclusive and more inconvenient reality can be known and appreciated for what it is.

Most leaders actually crave this kind of uncomfortable knowledge. I have coached more than one chief executive, for example, who has wrung his or her hands and exclaimed, 'If only they'd tell me the truth!' The yearning has nothing to do with uncovering malfeasance in order to punish the offender and demonstrate authority. Far from it. They want to know what's going on so they can fix it. It's not an exaggeration to say that some leaders even welcome mistakes. The reason being that it exposes weakness in the business that would otherwise go undetected, as well as providing the opportunity for all concerned to learn some lessons. One of my favourite management proverbs is: 'Leaders fail their people when they withhold the information those people need in order to succeed.' I think the proverb stands reversing. When people bury bad news or ply their leaders with sugar-coated versions of reality, the leader is weakened – and so, by implication, is the business.

Truth, in other words, is a resource. But truth is not the same as, or reducible to, information. The regular senior management team meeting will involve directors reporting on the news in their division or department, and that usually takes the form of information like supplier costs or sales figures or sickness absence or customers reached. And yet for all the information, the CEO can still feel uninformed, if not actively misled. As the prime decision-maker, what he or she needs to know is not the information per se, but what it really means. Again, that involves establishing a context where not only is it safe to speak the truth, but people are actively encouraged to bring the reality into the room.

# 41

# WHEN YOU SHOUT, HOW HIGH DO THEY JUMP?

Last summer I found myself in the staff canteen of a Silicon Valley technology company. More precisely, I was in the canteen of another company it had just acquired. The reason for my involvement was to work with the senior management team, newly refashioned from the two OldCos, on their roles and responsibilities. During a break for lunch, which I was sharing with some of the guys from HR, the CEO walked in – the new CEO, as far as the people in the canteen were concerned, the CEO who had bought their business and overnight become their boss. It wasn't exactly like when a stranger walks into a rural pub, but the merest break in conversation was followed by a whisper that susurrated around the room.

Clearly, there is an aura that attaches to leaders. They are not just at the top of the organisation, a single tier above the directors; they inhabit a different category. All other hierarchical layers in the organisation might be distributed more or less evenly on top of each other, like the strata in a rock face, but the leader is perceived as sitting above the rock altogether.

Strangely, however, this aura has almost nothing to do with personality. Even if the leader is blessed with natural authority, it merely supplements the authority natural to the position. The position comes first and it's this that bestows the primary power. All leaders have this positional authority, even if only some have the natural kind. Positional authority is the authority that comes simply by virtue of being the leader. And so it was in Silicon Valley. The CEO took his place in the food queue, like anyone else, chatted with a colleague in front of him and went to sit down. A shrewd but self-effacing Swede in his late forties, wearing khakis and a checked shirt, he simply blended in. If you didn't know he was the CEO, you might have thought he was a manager in the software division or had some regional operations role. But he didn't, and people knew it. Furtive glances were directed his way until he'd finished eating and left.

If just by virtue of being the leader, the leader has this hold over people, then it's a hold that's there to be lost. In theory, he or she could retain it by doing nothing. It may have some disturbing political implications, but the sheer presence of a leader is often enough for people to be ready to obey. If one thinks of the mask-like qualities of dictators in certain lands, that is precisely how power is maintained: the leader serves as a blank screen upon which the people project an ideal figure. The less he or she does to interfere with this projection, the intenser it will be.

Equally disturbing is the consequence for leaders of businesses. For any words and deeds they choose will carry a risk. Rather than bolstering the authority that comes with the leader position, such words and deeds could just as easily go the other way. Essentially, they have to be better than doing or saying nothing. That's the bar to beat. Do you generally enhance the authority of your position or do you generally undershoot it? Would it be better, as a rule, to shut up?

The very fact of being a leader means you don't have to go over the top in asserting your will: you don't have to resort to command-and-control because your authority speaks for itself. Indeed, the more emphatic you are, the less secure you appear in your position. If they jump higher when you shout, it's not out of respect, but fear. Which doesn't mean reverting instead to a consensual style. That would be overcompensating. The point about positional authority is that it lies exactly halfway between the two. Let the position speak for itself. You are the boss. Nothing need be added or taken away. It's simply your place in the system.

Most advice to leaders overlooks this positional or systemic perspective. Generally, it takes a psychological approach, emphasising the character traits necessary to be an effective leader. I always think it must be daunting for leaders to read any of the abundant leadership material now on offer. By turns they are asked to be charismatic, strategic, visionary, engaging, focused, emotionally intelligent, adaptive, clear, energetic, dynamic, creative, risk-taking, responsible, outwards-facing, inwards-facing, inspiring, brave and consistent. Some of the literature verges on the mystical, speaking of 'Level 5 leadership' as if it were a rung just shy of Jesus or the Buddha. Perhaps to bring things back down to earth, there has been a recent fashion for 'authentic' leadership, as promoted by Rob Goffee at London Business School, for example, which reminds leaders to be human, flawed and real. And what I like about this is that it sits very well alongside the positional leadership I'm describing. Because the simple fact of being the leader lends you power, you don't need to add much to it. It frees you to be real, and more reality is exactly what most businesses need.

In effect, therefore, I'm praising my Silicon Valley CEO, taking his lunch and causing a muffled stir among his junior colleagues. He may have done nothing special to augment the positional authority that came with his newly acquired status as their boss, but nor did he take anything away. Remember, the potential that leaders have for disappointing their people is almost limitless. Better sometimes just to be the boss.

# ARE YOU 100% PRODUCTIVE 100% OF THE TIME?

Anyone who answers yes to this question is lying. Not because being 100 per cent productive 100 per cent of the time is impossible, but because if you were 100 per cent productive 100 per cent of the time, you wouldn't be reading this: you'd be being productive.

Or is that right? Does being productive preclude reading a book? In theory, reading could help you become more productive. It could help to refocus your efforts so that you might switch from 'doing things right' to 'doing the right things', to paraphrase Peter Drucker. True, while you're reading you are inputting rather than outputting, but all output not only makes Jack a dull boy, it also means Jack never refills his tank. In fact, reading, along with meditation and yoga, is listed among the activities involved in 'sharpening the saw', the seventh of the famous *7 Habits of Highly Effective People* detailed by Stephen R. Covey.

Effective, you may object, is not the same as productive. You can be productive without being effective; for example, you can produce lots of furniture, but fail to adapt it to the taste of your customers, leading to surplus inventory and associated overheads – which are the opposite of productive. The subtler question is whether without being productive you can be effective at all. An effective politician, say, has to produce policies and arguments. Without these he or she would have no material to work with. So being effective is being usefully productive.

What about the other part of the question – the 100 per cent of the time part? This is a book for business leaders, not robots, even if some of those leaders will use robots in their factories. Indeed, the very idea of the factory is that of a 24/7 operation, even if it can't be staffed by humans at such intensive levels, or if the factory itself will sometimes need to close for maintenance. As for those leaders, let's break the 100 per cent down. Take off 25 per cent for sleep, and another 25 per cent for weekends, holidays, family, friends, illness and random interruptions. That leaves 50 per cent of the time, or twelve of the twenty-four hours. That's not a short working day, of course, but it's about right for most modern leaders. How to optimise the twelve hours to be most productive and, of course, effective? Should they even work fewer hours, on the hypothesis that it's better to work less but more effectively?

Christopher Rodrigues, the former president and chief executive of Visa International, once gave a speech in which he literally added up the number of hours and days he had available to him in a year. He drew a triangle on a flip-chart and put this number at the triangle's apex. At the base he wrote another number, to represent all the hours and days available to the combined front-line staff of his organisation. Needless to say, it was many thousand times greater than the number at the top. Clearly, the total productivity of the junior staff massively outstripped his own. That was the reality. There was no way he could ever compete.

A resignation speech this was not. His point was about effectiveness, about the relationship between his available time and theirs. It was in this relationship that he could switch from being merely productive to becoming massively effective. How so? He defined his job as the boss as enabling, empowering and supporting the junior guys as much as he could. If he did that, he could act as a lever and shift the whole organisation. His status was best used not by being as productive as possible on his own stuff, because that would always have a pretty low limit, but by using his relationship with his staff as a multiplier.

It's an idea that goes against some of our accepted ideas about effective leadership. We tend to think that the effective leader is someone who personally does a lot, someone who makes things happen directly, someone who controls the pyramid from the top. But Rodrigues ended his speech by turning the flip-chart upside down. The effective leader, he was suggesting, is a phenomenon you could only infer from an effective organisation. If your organisation was effective, it meant the boss was doing his or her best to help others do their job. The boss uses his or her limited resources most effectively by freeing up the resources of others.

What does that look like in practical terms? There are certain things that only the boss can do, and as a general rule the boss should stick to doing what only the boss can do. Doing anything else eats into the margin of effectiveness. And the three main things that only the boss can do are 1) make the biggest decisions; 2) resolve the blockages; 3) act as the most credible representative of the organisation to an outside audience. Of these three, it's the middle one that has the greatest bearing on the organisation's effectiveness. Things get gummed up in organisations mainly for reasons of politics, which is another name for business reality. Even apparently operational blockages, like the lorries arriving late at the depot, or the hotel running out of bottled water, often have 'political' causes at their root to do with things like one department not trusting another. This is precisely why strategies are so feeble in the face of reality. Most of the politics is more overt, of course, often revolving around a clash of egos. In all cases, the politics diverts energy from the work, and when that happens, the effectiveness drops too. What the boss can do is use his or her authority to refocus people on the job. Then the work can flow again.

In short, being 100 per cent productive 100 per cent of the time may be as undesirable as it is impossible. The point is to be effective, and to use one's position in the organisation to lever as much power from that organisation as possible.

# 43

# ARE YOU LONELY ENOUGH?

For some years, I ran a regular workshop entitled 'The Loneliness of the Internal Consultant' (the phrase alluded to *The
Loneliness of the Long-Distance Runner*, which was both a novel
and a film). The point of the workshop was twofold. First,
providing a home where internal consultants from various
large organisations could meet kindred spirits. For consulting
from the inside can indeed be a lonely business. These internal
consultants often found the demand for their services smaller
than the supply they so eagerly had to offer. Not being part
of the core business meant their authority was circumscribed.
Not being external meant they appeared less impartial and
sometimes less credible. Cheaper to hire they may have been
than those external equivalents, but of course that meant they
didn't get paid so well. Their loneliness wasn't always much
fun.

The second point of the workshop, however, was to turn
this loneliness into an advantage. Instead of trying to be loved
by their internal clients, these consultants were encouraged to
keep their distance, to rigorously maintain their independence.
Loneliness could be reframed as a professional asset. While it
may be true that clients, internal or otherwise, like to be told
what they want to hear, it's even truer that being told what
they need to hear offers the firmer basis for respect. Consultants slightly weaken themselves when they're ingratiating,

just as clients slightly despise themselves for accepting the consultant's flattery. The more external these internal consultants became in spirit, the better.

But loneliness isn't the sole preserve of consultants, internal or external. It has become a commonplace to cite the loneliness of the leader. Implicit is the idea that the leader's loneliness is bad. There's only one CEO as opposed to a team of them, which makes the CEO feel isolated. As CEO, you can talk to your life partner or your executive coach, but the top job is solitary by definition. To some degree you are compensated by the higher salary you draw, but still. For all the talk about 'leadership' as opposed to 'leaders', there's really only one person, alone in all his or her glory.

So the CEO and the internal consultant have more in common than they thought. And just as the internal consultant must strive to maintain detachment, so too must the CEO. This is the point I'll develop here.

'CEO' stands for chief executive officer, a title which suggests the role can be reduced to making the crunch decisions. The 'executive' part of 'chief executive officer' gives that role a highly operational air. A good CEO, however, is much more than an operational figure placed at a higher level. She or he has to lead, and part of leading is about not letting yourself get entangled in what you lead, not overly 'executing'. In the language of the management guru Ron Heifetz, you have to get off the dance floor and onto the balcony. Or, like an internal consultant, you have to stand back and watch what's going on from an objective point of view.

One of the best ways of understanding this objective stance, this valuable loneliness, is through a technique I was once taught by a colleague. He simply called it 'Conversations'. The technique started from the premise that one of the principal activities in an organisation is attending meetings, and because meetings are made up of conversations, if you can improve your skill in conversations, you can improve your meetings, and so improve a substantial part of the organisation's activity. And the way to improve a conversation is to make sure each of the following four stances is adopted during it:

1. proposing
2. opposing
3. following
4. commenting

A conversation that doesn't have this balance of elements won't go so well. Where there are people just proposing ideas, as in a brainstorm, there's no grounding in the facts. The proposing needs to be opposed or challenged to bring it down to earth. So the opposing role is key. But if in a conversation you only have proposing and opposing, it's going to end in deadlock. An irresistible force meets an immovable object. At least one of the proposed ideas must be followed if things are to move on. Once the proposal has been satisfactorily opposed or challenged, following it is essential.

Generally, we think the role of the leader is in the proposing. Obviously it's not in the following, and it wouldn't be appropriate for a leader to always adopt the opposing role. The leader should be a plus in the business, not a minus. If anyone plays the opposing role, it's typically those in operations who are more sensitive to capacity constraints on delivery. However, there is a fourth function – that of 'commenting'. The commenting role is vital as a sense-check on the whole, in order to put everything into perspective. Someone in the conversation has to introduce the wider view, to voice the heli-copter perspective, to encompass the larger reality in which the business sits as opposed to its narrow strategic context.

The helicopter or meta position is a lonely one, and it's where consultant and CEO merge. In a strange way, the CEO also stands outside the business he or she runs, even as he or she is the most integral part of it. There's a critically non-exec-utive aspect to the chief executive role, and it lies in 'comment-ing' on the conversation as a whole. In tangible terms it's the CEO when he or she is in the meeting as the chair. The chair's role isn't really to propose but to balance all the views that have been expressed, sum them up and reframe them before proceeding to any 'executive' decision.

As a business leader, you might occasionally lament your own loneliness. But the paradox is that you have to be outside the business you're so fundamentally inside. Otherwise, you become nothing more than the chief executive officer, and leadership is different from that. Being on the outside means holding the biggest picture of all, a picture in which as much external reality is included as possible.

# 44

# DOES THE AUTOPILOT
# NEED A REST?

It's easy to misread this question. It's not: 'Do you need a rest, and therefore should you switch on the autopilot?' No, it's asking whether the autopilot itself needs a break. The key point being that leaders, just like those lower down the hierarchy, spend rather too much time on automatic and rather too little making conscious choices. True, the automatic behaviour helps the brain to rest between moments of exertion, but the brain can rest too much in automatic mode.

Several factors conspire to produce such automatic behaviour. The main one by far is the diary. Picture the senior executive who walks into the office in the morning and asks her or his assistant, 'What am I doing today?' The assistant dutifully lists the day's appointments. Meeting at 8.00 with Sales. Conference call at 9.30 with Asia. Catch-up at 11.30 with the guys on the transformation project. Briefing at 12.00 on the agenda for the annual conference. Car to the airport at 13.00. And so on. The diary has a momentum of its own, often more forceful than anything around it. It's like a daily set of electronic commandments with which all too many leaders comply.

Almost as insidious as the diary is a factor that is largely a consequence of it: tiredness. There is a silent epidemic of fatigue among the world's senior executives. This is the demographic affected by jet lag, back-to-back meetings, handheld devices constantly receiving messages and a personal life implacably calling for the attention it never properly gets. The tiredness of the modern executive is a phenomenon that strangely parallels that of menial workers at the other end of the salary scale, and it can produce a similarly automated reaction. Sometimes success is simply getting through the day.

The third, and least tangible, factor that leads to automatism among leaders is what could be called the 'discourse' of business. Having arrived, tired, in the meeting required by the diary, the executive finds him- or herself in an environment with a well-established set of rules. These rules govern the language that can be used, the behaviour that is expected, who will be listened to, and the concerns that are judged to be most valid. Together these add up to the discourse of the business in question, the cultural norms and accepted way of doing things. To newcomers the discourse will seem a bit odd, like having dinner with a family you don't know very well. But over time, the discourse becomes normal. And as it becomes normal, so the effort required to decipher and adapt to it lessens. The consequence again is a kind of automatic reaction whereby those concerned reproduce the discourse rather than think independently. It also inures them to reality in that this set mode of operating causes leaders to see only what fits with their routine way of framing things.

These three factors – the diary, tiredness, and the business 'discourse' – bind together to form a sort of raft on which leaders will sometimes glide through the days at work. Truly conscious action, something that cuts across the flow of things, becomes a rarity. Often 'executives' are merely 'executing' what that flow had already prescribed. So what to do about it?

Ask the talented people in any organisation where they get their energy and ideas from, and more often than not they will cite things outside of work. A film they saw, an adventure they went on, a book they read, a podcast they downloaded, a phrase overheard. What these things have in common is that they interrupt that flow of everyday life. They are square pegs in the round hole of existence, and they have the effect of waking up a faculty in us that is mostly dormant, the faculty for seeing things afresh. It's this faculty that is so precious in business, because it's the source of innovation. True, businesses can't innovate all the time: most of the activity has to be consistent and effective delivery. But the remaining percentage is what's required to stop the delivery taking over and putting this rarer faculty to sleep.

It's not hard for business leaders to agree they should take more time out to have atypical experiences that might stimulate the brain in new ways. What is hard, however, is getting them to do it. This is precisely because those automatic forces – especially the diary – militate against it. What's more, the desire to keep doing the same is a lot more powerful than the desire to do something different, no matter what people say.

A classic and I think still effective remedy is what I call not the 'diary check', where you simply run through your appointments, figuring out where you have to be, when and with whom, but the 'diary chuck', where you chuck appointments out of the diary to make space for the things you know are more valuable. I say it's classic because it relies on the well-known distinction between the urgent and the important: the urgent always gets in the way of the important and the result is short-termism or constant 'fire-fighting'. There's also abbreviating meetings from an hour to forty-five minutes.

Where I've seen this done, the meetings have generally not suffered; it also helps to break the syndrome of meetings simply filling the time allotted. Other tips include holding meetings in different offices from your own; inviting in people you wouldn't normally invite; even just going for a walk. In all cases, the point is to cause an interruption to the automatic behaviour that keeps the business going but stops it from being alive to fresh ideas.

# 45

# ARE YOUR DECISIONS A SCIENCE OR AN ART?

Joe is chief executive of a large American telecoms firm. He is small-framed, as wiry as the silver-rimmed spectacles he favours, and dresses in an immaculate grey suit with all buttons fastened. Aged fifty, his skin appears paper-dry, and already considerably lined. He speaks only as much as it is necessary to speak in a given situation. His office is echoey from the lack of personal effects, and his desk never occupied by anything more than a computer and a phone.

Josh is managing director of a business that sits within one of Canada's major engineering companies. He is six foot five and about eighteen stone. Sometimes he'll sport a beard, or half a beard. He almost never stops talking and even as he talks he's usually on one of his two handheld devices, texting or emailing or tweeting. And when he talks, it's as likely to be about his kids or his ambitions to be a boat builder, as the business. Technically, he's based in Toronto, but he seems to be everywhere, all the time.

Joe and Josh are two clients that I know well and have worked with over a number of years. Besides the egregious external differences, what sets them apart from each other is the way they make decisions.

Not surprisingly, it will be on a strictly scientific basis that

Joe decides. For example, when he was appointed to the top job, he made some decisions about the make-up of his top team. His HR director – I'll call her Jane – was a woman of fifty-eight. Jane's husband, her last remaining family, had recently died from prostate cancer, and she was on bereavement leave in Toronto, the city they had moved to just three years earlier for her to take up the HR director role. The date for her return to work would fall just under a year before she was due to retire. Joe called her in during her leave period, and told her she'd have no job when she returned, so that effectively her retirement had already begun. He explained that her skill-set did not match the strategy he had for HR going forward, and that he'd already engaged headhunters to find her replacement. Jane left his office in tears, bereft for a second time.

Josh is the opposite. Little science ever applies; for him, decision-making is an art. So in the aftermath of the 2008 financial crisis, Josh went to his bosses to persuade them it was time to expand his business. The engineering industry worldwide might have been in the doldrums, but he had a gut feeling that for him and his division, things could be different. He was arguing for extra investment capital, asking permission to expand his organisation to more than twice its size. What was his evidence? He didn't have much, but he made his pitch with such charm and affability, such boyish optimism and ambition, that it was hard to resist. It was just such qualities that had always made him a hit with customers, and they knew it. With the right people, he said, he could shift the world; you can't succeed without capacity, so build the capacity and the business will follow. The resources were approved.

Between Joe and Josh, who made the better decision? Or,

rather, whose decision was made on the sounder basis? Joe, because he excluded the human factors, and put the operational effectiveness of the business first? Or Josh, because he didn't get bogged down in the analysis, and exhibited an infectious energy that got people behind him, going against the grain like a revolutionary hero?

As it turned out, neither Joe nor Josh was vindicated. Both were caught out. The trouble with Joe's eminently rational, 'scientific' decision was not that it wasn't right for the business, but that people got wind of it. The lack of compassion he had displayed towards Jane translated into wariness. People felt on their guard around him. This meant that the strategy Joe had so planfully devised for the business was something the other directors could feel only tepid about, in case they too were deemed unfit to pursue it. Which meant in turn that Joe just couldn't get the traction needed to move the organisation at anything like the pace he had intended. As for Josh, he commandeered the company shopping cart and made dozens of hires. He took his conscripts on team-building events and got them fired up about the new territories they were to conquer. They adored him and pledged their allegiance. Yet after six months, when the promised contracts still weren't coming in, the initial adrenalin started to ebb. People opted for 'working from home', and one or two left for employment elsewhere. A year in, and Josh had to fire 60 per cent of the crew he'd signed up. It was all terribly emotional.

From this cautionary tale there are two conclusions to draw. The first is obvious. When it comes to decision-making, you need a balance of science and art. Choosing one at the expense of the other is to operate with one eye. The second conclusion bears out my theme of the importance of reality over strategy. Despite their manifold differences, Joe and Josh shared the same weakness in the form of an infatuation with the future, an obsession with vision, a harping-on about strategic opportunities. In their fixation with strategy, neither of them took enough account of the present reality. In Joe's case, this was the reality of another human being's plight; in Josh's case, the commercial reality of the market.

There's another aspect worth touching on before I finish. In an academic paper quoted by Jonah Lehrer on decision-making, Aner Sela (University of Florida) and Jonah Berger (University of Pennsylvania) make the following remarks:

> Our central premise is that people use subjective experiences of difficulty while making a decision as a cue to how much further time and effort to spend. People generally associate important decisions with difficulty. Consequently, if a decision feels unexpectedly difficult, due to even incidental reasons, people may draw the reverse inference that it is also important, and consequently increase the amount of time and effort they expend.

What's interesting is that both Joe and Josh did something slightly different from what the paper is suggesting; they mistook a difficult decision for an easy one. This was because the strategy they had each settled on – to remodel the HR function, to grow the business – led them to treat decisions along the way as comparatively minor. Their respective decisions to sack the HR woman, and to hire staff, weren't given the importance they were due, and were taken lightly. And they were due importance because in both cases there was a significant reality in evidence: the woman's grief; unfavourable market conditions.

So perhaps the practical advice that follows is first to weigh up how important the decision you're about to take actually is. Don't let yourself agonise over whether you want vanilla or chocolate ice-cream, because it doesn't really matter. Do give serious thought to sacking a new widow near retiring age, or to hiring employees you don't have work for, even if it means laying your strategy aside while you face these more taxing realities.

# 46

# WHAT DO YOU TELL YOURSELF?

I will tell you about someone I coached, but not without disguising the person in question, for the sake of confidentiality. The point, in any case, is not the individual, but the syndrome, if I can use that word, from which this person suffered. Though if 'syndrome' makes it sound like a rare affliction, nothing could be further from the truth. What I'm referring to is a lack of self-awareness, a lack surprisingly common among business leaders, despite their level in the organisation. A lack, moreover, that may well be a personality defect, but more importantly, in this context, creates a risk for the business they lead.

So, this man ran the operations division of a Dutch consumer-electronics retailer. The products were aimed at the volume end of the market: relatively cheap goods of not especially high quality, but with mass appeal. One of the consequences of the poor quality was that customers would complain of appliances breaking down – warranties were offered only for twelve months, and were expensive to extend. After a management reshuffle, repairs and their outsourcing also came under this man's remit. This made a pretty big job even bigger, with the potential for numerous disgruntled punters.

As part of my coaching process, I would shadow him on the job – not as a constant companion, more dipping in to the occasional meeting to observe how he operated. Admittedly, my presence might have distorted his behaviour, but making coaching purely scientific is always going to be a stretch. Besides, after the first few meetings, it came to feel reasonably normal for all concerned to have me there – though never without a routine joke about me being his probation officer.

The main meeting I attended was that of the senior management team on a Monday morning. My coaching client was one of the 'big four' divisional directors, along with a Corporate Affairs director for support functions, and a CEO. This CEO chaired the meetings in classic style, going round the various directors for updates and issues in their area (the fact that this is a hopeless way to run a meeting is another matter: an exchange between two people doesn't need to have everyone else present). Whenever it came to my man – let's call him David – there was a suppressed, but collective, sense of dread. David had a habit of going on and on, never quite getting to the point. It was exacerbated by the fact that he chose his words with pedantic precision, making for agonising gaps between them that left his colleagues in a suspense that was never justified by the word upon which he eventually alighted. Throughout his extended disquisitions, he'd be looking down at the backs of his hands or up into the sky. And as if all that weren't bad enough, he'd use his slot not to give punchy information about the Ops division he ran, but to muse philosophically on the nature of consumer desire. It's a wonder he wasn't throttled.

Hence the coaching. The CEO had called me in, saying David needed to up his game. The Ops division felt rudderless. David behaved at his own divisional management team meetings in the same way he behaved at SMT. There was no 'grip'. The background being that David had been in a strategy role, which suited his intellectual nature, but was moved to Ops because of a sudden vacancy and a paucity of other candidates. He was a square peg in a round hole, but the CEO felt he might be developable in this grittier part of the business (I think she had a soft spot for him). He'd been sent on the appropriate training, but it hadn't made much difference. Coaching was a last resort.

With David's permission, I did what any coach would do at the start of an engagement, and sought feedback on him from his colleagues – peers, juniors and the CEO. I also asked him to answer the same questions I put to them, about his strengths and weaknesses. Not surprisingly, there was a gulf between the two. Overwhelmingly, the feedback said things like 'Nice guy, but he's on another planet,' 'We want it to work out for him, but he's just not engaging with the business,' 'His heart's in the right place, but he bores us to death.' David's self-assessment, by contrast, revealed a man who thought he was good at engaging with his colleagues, had a clear vision of where the business needed to go, but wasn't sure whether he was putting enough time into understanding the underlying issues. In other words, he thought he should be doing more of exactly what his colleagues thought he should be doing less of.

When I shared the feedback with him – and I did it as carefully as I could, while not pulling any punches – he was momentarily confused, perhaps a little shocked. Then he tried ascribing the anonymised comments to whomever might have said them, with a view to dismissing those comments as subjective or self-interested. Next he switched into analytical mode, quizzing me on the methodology I had used to gather the data and how robust it was. Finally, he tried changing the subject, before going round the loop again. I was holding up a mirror, and it was as if he'd never seen his reflection before. Perhaps it was too much too soon. The mixture of defensiveness and denial that characterised his reaction suggested to me that he could take the truth only in quarter teaspoonfuls, and I'd given him too large a dose.

Nevertheless, there was never going to be any progress without building up some self-awareness on his part, making him aware of the reality of how he came across. If you're blind to a weakness, how can you possibly address it? The more important point being that we tell ourselves stories about ourselves which are sometimes totally at variance with the perception of us held by others. If we can see ourselves as others see us, and interrupt those stories, there's a fighting chance of overcoming whatever it is that's keeping us weak.

With or without the support of a coach, it's always worth asking yourself what other people would say about you. It's a way of stepping outside of yourself, even adopting the detached position I talked about in chapter 43, on loneliness. From this perspective, you start to appreciate how you're perceived, and, as the adage has it, perception is reality. Not to put too fine a point on it, it will be the basis on which you succeed or fail in your job.

# 47

# WHAT WOULD YOU TELL YOUR THERAPIST?

I have been reading *The Examined Life* by Stephen Grosz. He is a psychoanalyst and the book consists of case studies of his patients. In one chapter he suggests that the most difficult patients are not necessarily the psychotic or the abusive, but the secretive. These are the people who won't tell him they are alcoholics, for example. What's the point in going into psychoanalysis if you don't disclose facts of such import?

Grosz reminded me of my own analyst saying, 'I can only analyse what you bring into the room'. Psychoanalysts and therapists work hard to create conditions safe enough for patients to feel they can bring anything. They listen carefully, they make no judgements and they keep strictly to time. But it can still be hard for a patient to let go. For all the safety mechanisms in place, the analyst is another adult, and confessing can induce feelings of shame.

Here and there in this book, and specifically in the last chapter, I have talked about clients I have coached. Although coaching differs from psychoanalysis in a number of ways, there are certain overlaps. One of the most important is this question of what the client chooses to talk about versus what he or she hides. Unless the reality is brought into the room, there's only so much the coach can do; any personal development strategy based on partial reality will be proportionally enfeebled. Indeed, as I've been arguing throughout this book, reality is more powerful than strategy of any ilk – market strategy, brand strategy, and even, as here, personal development strategy. Better always to take account of as much reality as possible and cut your strategy cloth accordingly, rather than doing it the other way round, and praying that reality will somehow play out as your strategy intended.

I once coached the CEO of a large European service-delivery business. She was a powerful figure, with a fine intellect and a strong sense of purpose. I was especially struck by how candid she was with her colleagues when I saw her in action at the meetings or away-days she asked me to facilitate. One winter, for example, there had been heavy snow across the Continent and it had disrupted much of their business. In front of her colleagues she admitted to making some poor decisions as part of what they called their 'emergency response process'. She genuinely took the blame, and her colleagues respected her for it.

In our coaching sessions we would frequently return to the same theme – the fact that her intellect was as much a weakness as a strength. It was an intellect that allowed her to process complex information with extraordinary rapidity. It meant she could instantaneously provide a way in meetings of reframing the problem so it became newly thinkable. It saved her from being caught out by awkward questions from shareholders, staff and others. But together these also added up to a downside. Like a lead runner, she would get too far ahead of the pack behind her, and they would lose motivation. She had it all worked out, so what was the need for them? Once or twice I saw her pose a question to the team and not wait for an answer – an answer she gave with great clarity and insight. And yet she was sufficiently candid and self-aware to apologise and then restrain herself while the others grappled in their own less superhuman way with the issue at hand.

After one such session, I found myself in the lift with an assistant director. I told her I'd been with the CEO and her instant reaction was, 'She's a f***ing bully.' I was shocked – not by the language, but by the possibility that the woman I'd been coaching might have this other side to her. After the shock, I rationalised it by saying to myself that this was sour grapes. The woman in the lift must hold a personal grudge against the CEO; perhaps she had been slighted, perhaps she was envious. But no. I was to find out later that there was indeed a wide perception of the CEO as a bully, and stories started coming to light about her intimidating junior staff who came to present to the SMT, for example, or throwing her weight around with the IT function. What the assistant director declared in the lift was, in effect, common knowledge.

But this common knowledge was not known to me. I wasn't an insider in the organisation. I was an outsider and my only real source of knowledge about the CEO was the CEO herself. Perhaps I should have been more intuitive and picked up on her bullying tendencies in our sessions; but I personally never felt bullied by her, and it's quite a good rule of thumb for a coach that what your client makes you feel is how he or she makes other people in the organisation feel too. But that's not really the point. The CEO herself should have introduced the subject. She didn't have to confess to being a bully. She need only have said that she was perceived as such by a number of people, or that she had developed such a reputation. It's just about conceivable, of course, that she wasn't aware of such perceptions. It's also possible, though I think unlikely, that she didn't trust me enough as a coach to discuss it. I think the truth was that she was too ashamed to have it acknowledged and discussed. So although she had hired me as a coach, she had drawn some invisible lines around me, defining what could and couldn't be discussed. In this sense, she was perhaps seeking personal affirmation rather than personal development, and excluding reality served her purposes best.

The case study I have offered verges on the lurid. Nevertheless it carries a sober message. Like anyone else, business leaders are sensitive to criticism. You don't get to be a leader without being in some ways superior to those around you: for the god to acknowledge that its feet are made of clay can be a challenge. And yet all leaders have their flaws. The question is how they manage them. For flaws come in two flavours, the acceptable and the unacceptable. In my experience, leaders will readily concede that they don't spend enough time reflecting, for example, or that they rely too much on too few sources for their information. What causes them to be more reluctant in laying out their flaws is where shame attaches to any one of them. But it's precisely in these more shameful flaws that the most important areas for development lie. So whether it's with a coach or not, I urge you as a leader to address head on the thing of which you're least proud – you're unlikely to be the only one with flaws, after all. Then you can move on with your head a little higher.

# 48

# WHAT WILL THEY SAY WHEN YOU'VE GONE?

I spent yesterday with the board of a major charity, helping them figure out their long-term direction of travel. The chief executive had just informed them that he will be stepping down in a few months' time. Obviously this means he won't be accompanying them on that onward journey. But it doesn't mean he has no stake in it, nor that upon his departure he'll be instantly forgotten. Unwittingly or not, every leader leaves a legacy. The question is how to shape it.

The first lesson is that leaving the shaping of your legacy until the moment you announce your resignation is leaving it too late. No sooner has the message of departure been transmitted, than the power of the leader starts to wane, and interest in him or her to ebb. It's not malice or pent-up disloyalty that prompts people to diminish the leader in this way. It's that they need to redraw their mental map of the organisation they work in; to disinvest in the current leader to make space for investing in the next; even to experience some temporary relief from being under the control of a certain individual. But the fact remains that announcing your resignation means ceding a significant amount of power (one reason, incidentally, why I believe notice periods at this level should be as short as possible). The phrase 'The King is dead, long live the

King' is far more enabling to the life of the organisation than 'The King is dying.' So legacy-shaping has to begin much earlier in the leader's tenure, when people are still listening – remember Jack Welch insisting that the leader's first priority is to groom the successor.

There's a fashion for claiming that there's nothing so decisive for a leader's authority and reputation than his or her actions in the first ninety or hundred days in office. Up to a point, this is true. Early actions set the tone, but they are not the be-all and end-all. If during those first few months no crisis occurs, then arguably the leader hasn't been called upon to show his or her true mettle. The reaction to crisis will likely make a far deeper impression on colleagues than the responses to the relatively blander conditions before it. One thinks of George W. Bush getting the message about 9/11 and continuing to read to schoolchildren.

I'll develop this example from American politics. When a decade later we learned that the man behind 9/11 had been killed on orders from President Obama, we formed a different kind of impression. Obama was well beyond the first hundred days, and his profile had been established as an urbane, intellectual policy-maker under attrition from unregenerate, red-blooded Republicans. The fact that he'd commanded Bin Laden's assassination revealed something altogether less cerebral and more kinetic, characteristics that will become a critical component of a legacy that would have otherwise been more one-dimensional. I'm not insinuating that Obama had Bin Laden killed for the sake of his own legacy. The point is that a decisive, positive act that flies in the face of people's expectations will leave as deep an impression as anything done in the normal run of things. There's a negative version of the same logic, of course, in the case of Tony Blair's intervention in Iraq. Just as urbane as Obama Blair may have been, but Iraq is what he'll be remembered – and widely reviled – for. In all cases, it's about making a lasting impression, and a lasting impression is formed more at moments of drama than during business as usual. How you respond to crisis will be decisive.

This isn't to say that how you conduct business as usual has no bearing. After all, there'll only be so many crises, by definition. Your legacy will also be informed by your general character during ordinary times – your character as opposed to your performance, that is. When people look back on leaders past, it's not often that they'll cite the profit figures during the years of his or her tenure, nor the acquisitions, divestments, governance arrangements or reporting cycle, unless such things themselves brought on a drama. Yes, you need to leave the business in a better condition than you found it: that is the basic and indisputable requirement, and if you don't sign up to that at the beginning of your reign, you probably shouldn't sign up at all. Your setting and following a sensible strategy to do so is a given, but it won't leave as lasting an impression as the character of the leader. That's what lingers in the mind of your legatees, not the strategy plans from three, five or ten years before.

The departing charity chief executive is a man of good character. Not goody-goody, but good. Maybe you'd expect that in the boss of a charity, but I've come across more than one senior person in other charities with an ego as big as anything you'd find in the private sector. Charity and humility by no means automatically go together. 'Good character' sounds old-fashioned and not very business school, but in terms of leaving a legacy, it's what matters most.

This talk of who the leader is brings us full circle from the first chapter of this book, where I spoke about 'who' the business is. In both cases I have emphasised identity and character, because I believe it's these that create a deeper impression on customers and employees than strategies ever will.

# EPILOGUE

This book, with its various questions, has been set up as a 'reality test': the point of taking such a test is that it should help business leaders prepare for what the world is actually like rather than what their strategy would like it to be like. I have had privileged access to a vast range of businesses, and the stories I've shared in this book prove there's an equally vast range of factors that impact on a given enterprise, of which those taken into account by a strategy represent only the merest fraction. It's a question therefore of opening one's eyes to the wider panorama of business reality, and preparing oneself accordingly.

The questions I've explored are designed to help with that, but they're not a finite set. There will be many more questions that could be asked in a similar vein, and this is something I'd very much encourage. I have two tips on how to do this. The first is to put yourself in the position of a layperson who's more likely to ask less specialist but more incisive questions. The second is to delay devising any strategy until you've asked and answered them: it will be far more robust. Neither has to be done in isolation. My suggestion would be to take the questions from this book, or others you may generate along similar lines, and use them as the basis for a working session with your colleagues. I think you will get a lot further into the reality of your business than asking the more typical strategy questions about market share, diversification, and so on. Treat this book as a spur to look at things as they are, and make your decisions accordingly.

My final reflection is a personal one. I have been a consultant now for some years. In the early days, I used to walk into the client's office with a host of models and tools up my sleeve, and some very earnest thoughts about the strategic context. What I've come to realise is that these assets I was bringing are easily sourced elsewhere or indeed replicated by the client themselves. In other words, they add little value. What clients value much more is a straight conversation, without the PowerPoint slides or the triangles drawn on flip-charts. What works best, in other words, is not me being 'strategic' but me being real.

# FURTHER READING

Richard Beckhard and R. T. Harris, *Organizational Transitions: Understanding Complex Change* (Addison-Wesley, 1977)

Jim Collins and Jerry I. Porras, *Built to Last: Successful Habits of Visionary Companies*, 2nd revised edition (Random House, 1998)

Stephen R. Covey, *The 7 Habits of Highly Effective People*, reprinted edition (Simon & Schuster, 2004)

Peter Drucker, *Essential Drucker*, second revised edition (Butterworth-Heinemann, 2007)

Jules Goddard and Tony Eccles, *Uncommon Sense, Common Nonsense: Why Some Organisations Consistently Outperform Others* (Profile Books, 2012)

Rob Goffee and Gareth Jones, *Why Should Anyone Be Led by You? What It Takes to Be an Authentic Leader* (Harvard Business School Press, 2006)

Noah J. Goldstein, Steve J. Martin and Robert B. Cialdini, *Yes! 50 Secrets from the Science of Persuasion* (Profile Books, 2007)

Stephen Grosz, *The Examined Life: How We Lose and Find Ourselves* (Chatto and Windus, 2013)

Ron Heifetz and Marty Linsky, *Leadership on the Line: Staying Alive Through the Dangers of Leading* (Harvard Business School Press, 2002)

Bert Hellinger and Gabriele ten Hövel, *Acknowledging What Is: Conversations with Bert Hellinger* (Zeig, Tucker & Theisen Inc., 1999)

Spencer Johnson, *Who Moved My Cheese? An Amazing Way to Deal with Change in Your Work and in Your Life*, reprinted edition (Vermilion, 1999)

David H. Maister, *Managing the Professional Service Firm*, new edition (Free Press, 2003)

Michael E. Porter, *Competitive Strategy: Techniques for Analyzing Industries and Competitors*, new edition (Free Press, 2004)

Richard Rumelt, *Good Strategy, Bad Strategy: The Difference and Why It Matters* (Profile Books, 2011)

Peter M. Senge, *The Fifth Discipline: The Art and Practice of the Learning Organization*, second revised edition (Random House, 2006)

?Whatif!, *Sticky Wisdom: How to Start a Creative Revolution at Work* (Capstone, 2002)

# READER'S NOTES

_____

_____

_____

_____

_____

_____

_____

_____

_____

_____

_____

_____

_____

_____

_____

_____

_____

_____

_____

# ACKNOWLEDGEMENTS

Thank you, as ever, to Stephanie Ebdon, my agent, and Daniel Crewe, my editor. You are simply the best.

I'd also like to express my gratitude to the many colleagues and partners from whom I've learned so much.

# INDEX

**A**

accountability 137, 182–6, 217

acquisitions 12–13, 24

adding value 34–8

agendas 34–5

alumni effect 149

Amazon 24, 25

ambiguity 118–19, 141–3, 144–5

analytical skills 176

Apple 70–1, 90, 91, 92, 98–9, 99, 100

Arab Spring 52, 109

arbitrary decisions 32

Aristotle 86

Asian financial crisis 21, 22

aspirations 50

AT Kearney 64

attitudes 40, 163–4
   to money 43–6

atypical experiences 205–6

aura 64–5, 191–4

Australia 51–2

'authentic' leadership 193

authority 115, 191–4, 198

automatic behaviour 203–6

automation 129

**B**

bad citizens 160–4

BAE 52

Bain 63

banks 16, 49–50, 99, 127, 154, 156–7

Barclays 183, 185

BAT (British American Tobacco) 19–20, 21

Beckhard, Richard 40–1

behaviours 158, 159, 163–4
   automatic 203–6

beliefs 40, 110–11, 112

belonging 132–5, 137, 138, 140, 155

benign deception 187–90

Berger, Jonah 210

Bin Laden, Osama 51, 221

black sheep 138, 139

Blair, Tony 221–2

blockages 65, 119, 197–8
BMW 68, 69, 70, 71
Bohner, Gerd 93–4
bonding 65–7
Booz & Company 64
Boston Consulting Group 63
brand 23, 36, 37, 38, 62, 68–71,
    74, 75
  internal 165
  predictability 98–100
Branson, Sir Richard 47–8
Britain *see* UK
British American Tobacco *see*
    BAT
*Built to Last* (Collins and
    Porras, 1998) 18
'burning platform' 41–2
Bush, George W. 221
business, discourse of 204
business models 90–1
business relationships 84–7
business terms 90–2
businesses 7–8, 66
  family businesses 139
  founders 26–7, 29, 140
  founding moments 26–7,
    28
  identity 9–13, 72–5, 93–4,
    96–7, 222–3
  longevity 18, 20
  as only children 63–5
  performance 77–8, 155, 156

'pheromones' of 72–5
planning the end of 18–19,
    20, 21
in society 7–8, 22–5, 55–7
uniqueness 11–12, 75, 92,
    104
*see also* companies;
    corporations;
    organisations

**C**
Cadbury Schweppes 146
Cameron, David 123
capitalism 24, 35–6, 37–8,
    44–5, 106
case for change 41–2
Catholic Church of England
    and Wales 121, 123, 123–4
CEOs 176–7, 200–2
    *see also* accountability;
    leaders
change 40–1, 138–9
change management 40–2
chaos theory 28
character 193, 222–3
China 22–3, 52
Cisco, and Flip 12–13
Civil Service 122, 134–5
cognitive ability 175–6,
    217–18
Collins, Jim 18
comfort zone 158

commenting role 201–2

communism 24, 44

companies
  Japanese 22–3, 24–5, 74–5,
    165–6, 168
  loyalty to 147, 149, 165
  'pheromones' 72–5
  see also businesses;
    corporations

competitive advantage 66,
  107

competitors 1, 15, 36, 61,
  105–8, 111–12, 147

complexity 175, 217

connecting energy within
  organisations 65–7

consequences, unintended
  55–7

consultants 88–9, 91–2, 179,
  225
  internal 199–200, 202

consumption 38

context 19–20, 52–3, 89–90,
  101–4, 106

'Conversations' technique
  200–2

Conway 56–7

Le Cool 96–7

Le Corbusier 100

corporate death row 152–3

corporate social responsibility
  23

corporations
  Japanese 22–3, 24–5, 74–5,
    165–6
  Western 23–4, 25
  see also businesses;
    companies

costs 36
  of change 41
  of networking 84, 85

Covey, Stephen R. 195

Cravath, Swaine & Moore
  LLP 151, 153–4

creativity 11, 125

crises
  economic 16, 21, 22
  reaction to 221–2

culture, organisational 148–9,
  152, 154, 156–9, 188–90

curiosity 150

customer service 49, 81, 107

customers 2, 61, 71, 107,
  130–1, 180–1, 212
  adding 'meaning' to lives of
    37, 38
  and business identity 10, 11
  expectations of
    predictability 98–100
  and 'passion' for the
    product 77, 79
  relationships with 84–7
  sellers and 80–2
  and value 35, 37, 38

## D

data, ambiguity of 141–3,
    144–5
dead wood 151–5
death row, corporate 152–3
deception, benign 187–90
decision-making 117–19, 197,
    207–10, 225
decisions 32, 52–3, 210–11
delayering 49–50
democracy 25, 31–2, 109
demographic shifts 89–90
detachment 199–200, 215
'developing' countries 109
development 42
    of employees 148–9, 151,
        152, 154
    personal 216–19
dialogue 121–2, 123
Diamond, Bob 183–4, 184,
    185, 186
diaries 203, 204, 205–6
differentiation 92
digital technology 57, 62
disasters, avoiding 51–4
'discourse' of business 204
discretionary energy 78–9, 79
dismissals 26, 137, 138, 152–3,
    208, 209, 210–11
dissatisfaction with the
    present 41
dissent, 'obligation to' 188–9

diversity, lack of 134
doing the same thing 40
dress codes 132–4
Drucker, Peter 195
Duchamp, Marcel 103
Dyson 107–8
Dyson, Sir James 107

## E

Eastman, George 105–6
Eccles, Tony 110, 112
economic crises 16, 21, 22
effectiveness 66, 195–8
efficiency 152–3
employees
    development of 148–9, 151,
        152, 154
    getting rid of 137, 138,
        151–3
    going the 'extra mile' 78–9,
        137
    variability 78–9, 154–5
energy 41, 106, 154, 205
    connecting energy within
        organisations 65–7
    discretionary 78–9, 79
enough, 'how much is?' 47–50
enterprises, social worth 22–5
European Union 123
*Examined Life, The* (Grosz,
    2013) 216
expansion 153

expectations 98–100, 166
expenses, networking on 84, 85, 86, 86–7
experience 165–6
'extra mile' 78–9, 137

**F**
fairness, instinct for 45
families, organisations resembling 136–40
family businesses 139
*Far from the Tree* (Solomon, 2013) 30
fatigue 203–4
FCO (Foreign and Commonwealth Office) 126–7
'fire-fighting' 205
fitting in 132–5
Flip, Cisco and 12–13
Foreign and Commonwealth Office *see* FCO
founders 26–7, 29, 140
founding moments 26–7, 28
*Fountain* (Duchamp, 1917) 103
*Friendly Fire* (Snook, 2000) 185–6
Fujifilm 105–6, 107
future 2, 27, 41, 209–10, 214

**G**
give-and-take 154–5

globalisation 24, 54, 173
Goddard, Jules 110, 112
Goffee, Rob 193
*Good Strategy, Bad Strategy* (Rumelt, 2011) 105, 106
Goodwin, Fred 183–4, 186
Green, Sebastian 136–7
'grit in the oyster' 134–5
Grosz, Stephen 216
group identity 132–5
growth 11, 42, 47–8, 153
    Japan 22–3
    professional 148–9, 151, 152, 154

**H**
Haysom, Mark 182–3, 184
Heifetz, Ron 200
Hellinger, Bert 136–7, 138
hierarchy 137
hierarchy of needs 36–7
high street 53, 102
HMV 53
holistic view 55–7
Hoover 107–8
horizontal organisations 30–1, 32–3
'how much is enough?' 47–50

**I**
ideas, sources of 205–6

identity
    of businesses 9–13, 72–5,
        93–4, 96–7, 222–3
    group identity 132–5
    of leaders 171–2, 222–3
implementation 77–8
India 109
inequalities 44, 45
information 2, 149–50,
    189–90
Ingenious Media 73, 74
innovation 11, 61, 99–100, 106,
    125–6, 166, 205
    and context 101–4
    unpredicted 110–11
'institutional failure' 185
integrity 86–7
intellect 175–6, 217–18
intellectual capital 147
internal brand 165
internal consultants 199–200,
    202
Internet 24–5, 53
interpersonal skills 176
investment strategy 51–2
invisible market 111–12
inwards-facing organisations
    123, 124
Iraq 221–2
itches, organisational
    125–8

J
Japan 21, 22–3, 123
    companies 22–3, 24–5, 74–5,
        165–6, 168
Jaques, Elliott 175
'jobs for life' 147, 148

K
Kennedy's Sausages 39–40
'knowing when to go' 18–21
knowledge network 149–50
Kodak 105–6
Kongo Gumi 20–1

L
Lawrence, Stephen 185
leaders 2, 135, 157, 171–2
    appointing 165–6, 168
    authority 115, 191–4, 198
    automatic behaviour 203–6
    character 193, 222
    detachment 71, 200–2, 215
    early actions 221
    effectiveness 195–8
    as facilitators 33, 197–8
    flaws 219
    identity 171–2, 222–3
    intellect 175–6, 217–18
    legacies 220–3
    loneliness 200–2
    need to know the truth
        187–90

and 'noble lie' 141–5
performance 222
personalities 171–2
role 177, 185–6, 197, 200–2
seeing the big picture 7, 71,
    200–2
self-awareness 2–3, 212–15
setting the overall tone 186
taking responsibility 182–5
tiredness 203–4, 204
value added by 173–7
*see also* accountability;
    leadership; succession
leadership 145, 166, 177, 200
    'authentic' 193
    effective 195–8
    and the 'extra mile' 78–9
    styles 33, 192–3
    *see also* leaders
learning
    culture of 148–9, 152, 154
    from the past 2, 26–9, 138–9
Learning and Skills Council
    182–3
legacies of leaders 220–3
Lehrer, Jonah 210
lies, acceptable 141–5
loneliness 199–202
long-term trends 52–4
longevity, of businesses 18, 20
losing, organising not to lose
    15–17

love, seeking 178–81, 199
loyalty
    to the company 147, 149,
        165
    to the tribe 131

**M**
McKinsey & Company 63, 64,
    148, 149
Maister, David 85
margins 36, 49, 107
market 35–6, 61–2, 106,
    109–12, 134
market share 36, 106
Mars 146
Maslow, Abraham, hierarchy
    of needs 36–7
'meaning' 36–8
meetings 200–2, 205–6, 213
Metropolitan Police 185
Microsoft 90–1, 92, 102
Mikitani, Hiroshi 24
military strategy 51, 52
mission statements 15, 105–6
mistakes, repeating 2, 138–9,
    166
modernisation 23, 39
modernism 100, 102–3
money 43–6, 48, 179
Monitor 63–4, 65
monopolies 106
'myth of outsourcing' 56–7

**N**

NATO 72, 73, 74, 75
needs, hierarchy of 36–7
networking 84–7
Nike 56
'noble lie' 141–5
Northrop Grumman 52
'Not Invented Here' 119

**O**

Obama, Barack 123, 221
'one of us' 132–5
only children, businesses as
  63–5
openness, culture of 188–90
opportunities 53–4
organisation charts 123
  delayering 49–50
  restructuring 78, 126, 167
organisational culture 148–9,
  152, 154, 156–9, 188–90
organisational itches 125–8
organisations 2, 115–16, 120
  connecting energy within
    65–7
  default setting to expand
    153
  horizontal 30–1, 32–3
  inwards-facing 123, 124
  loyalty to 147, 149, 165
  organic nature 115–16, 120,
    134–5, 154–5

outwards-facing 122–3,
  124
'pheromonal' identity 73–4
and purpose 14–17
resembling families 136–40
restructuring 78, 126, 167
social footprints 55–7
as social systems 155
tribes within 130–1
upwards-facing 121–2, 123,
  124
values 18, 161
vertical 30–1, 32, 121–2
*see also* businesses;
  companies; corporations
outsourcing, 'myth of' 56–7
outwards-facing
  organisations 122–3, 124

**P**

passion 77, 79
past, learning from 2, 26–9,
  138–9, 166
pay, working ratio of boss to
  employee 173
people 2
  development 148–9, 151,
    154
  getting rid of 137, 138,
    151–3
  going the 'extra mile' 78–9,
    137

variability 78–9, 154–5
perception, as reality 215
perfection 2, 119–20
performance
 business 77–8, 155, 156
 individual 77–9, 133–4,
  134–5, 154–5
 leaders' 222
personal development 216–19
personalities 163, 171–2
'pheromones' of businesses
 72–5
Plato 144
playing the game 132–5
politics 78, 115, 153, 197–8
Porras, Jerry I. 18
Porter, Michael E. 61, 63
positional authority 191–4
Post-it notes 110–11
predictability 98–100, 109–12
present 27
 dissatisfaction with 41
price 36, 38, 70, 71, 106, 107
 and value 35, 92
private insights 110–11, 112
problem staff 151–5
processes 78
Proctor & Gamble 148
productive, being 195–7, 198
productivity 78, 154
products 36, 37, 38, 79, 101–2
 see also innovation

professional growth 148–9,
 151, 152, 154
profit 44
psychoanalysis 216
purpose 7–8, 14–17, 77, 131

**Q**
quality 35, 36, 38, 70, 71, 106
quality of life 24, 44
questions 2–4, 35, 161, 224–5

**R**
RACI charting 184–5
Rakuten 24–5
reality 116, 120, 163, 202, 215,
 224–5
 and the market 61–2, 109–12
 of others 80–3
 predicting 109–12
 strategy and 1–4, 12–13,
  49–50, 67, 188, 209–10,
  217, 224–5
 see also truth
reality test 2–4, 224–5
recognition 137
'Reinventing the Wheel'
 118–19
relationships
 with customers 84–7
 trust within 94–6
 within organisations 65–7
resignations 220–1

resources, competition for
51–2
respect 137, 138
responsibility 137, 182–6
corporate social 23
social 23, 55–7
restructuring 78, 126, 167
Rio Tinto 101
risk 44, 53–4
Rodenhauser, Tom 64
Rodrigues, Christopher 196–7
Room to Read 102
Royal Bank of Scotland 183–4
Rumelt, Richard 105, 106, 107

### S
saboteurs 2, 153
sacking people 26, 137, 138,
152–3, 208, 209, 210–11
Saudi Arabia, and change 42
seeing things afresh 205
Sela, Aner 210
self-awareness 2–3, 218–19
lack of 212–15
sellers, and customers 80–2
services 36, 37, 38
7 Habits of Highly Effective
People, The (Covey, 2004)
195
shame 216, 218–19
Shell 147–8
short-termism 205

sign of the times, being a
88–92
Skills Funding Agency see
Learning and Skills Council
Skoda 68, 69–70, 70, 71
Smith, Colin Rowland 76–7
Smith, R. R. (Robert Rowland)
76
Smith, R. W. 76
Snook, Scott 185–6
social responsibility 23,
55–7
social worth of enterprises
22–5
socialism 24
society, businesses in 7–8,
22–5, 55–7
Solomon, Andrew 30
spies 146, 147–8, 149–50
Starbucks 15
strategising, as discovery
process 110–11
strategy 105, 161, 168, 222
aimed at perfection 120
and context 52–3, 103–4
as fantasy 50, 105, 117–18
getting people to engage in
65–7
and implementation 77–8
investment strategy 51–2
military strategy 51, 52
preoccupation with 7, 77–8

and reality 1–4, 12–13,
    49–50, 67, 188, 209–10,
    217, 224–5
  time horizons for 52–3
succession 157, 165–6, 168,
    220–1
supermarkets, UK 106
symbols 158–9
synergy 129–30
'systemic failure' 185
systems 158

**T**
targets 48, 78
technological shifts 89–90
technologies, differentiating
    92
terms of business 90–2
think tanks 32–3
'tight/loose' framework
    115
time horizons 18–19, 52–3
*Time Out* 96, 97
tiredness 203–4, 204
trade secrets 146–7, 148, 150
trading skill 90–2
transparency 62, 82–3
trends, long-term 52–4
tribes 130–1
trust 43, 82–3, 94–6, 135, 158,
    165
truth, need to know 187–90

**U**
UK
  government use of
    consulting services 88–9
  inwards-facing 123, 124
  supermarkets 106
uncertainty 61, 109
unintended consequences 55–7
uniqueness 11–12, 75, 92, 104
unpredictability 61, 109
'up or out' policies 151–2
upwards-facing organisations
    121–2, 123, 124

**V**
value 35–8, 70, 84, 92
  adding 34–8, 173–7
  context-dependent 101, 103
value added 34–8, 173–7
values 18, 161
vertical organisations 30–1,
    32, 121–2
Virgin 47–8
visceral energies 41, 106
visible market 111–12
vision 18–19, 41, 209–10, 214

**W**
weaknesses 16, 107–8, 217–19
  making enough of 93–7
  *see also* self-awareness
Welch, Jack 221

Western corporations 23–4, 25
  appointing leaders 166
*Who Moved My Cheese?*
  (Johnson, 1999) 41
who you are
  businesses 9–13, 72–5, 93–4,
    96–7, 222–3
  leaders 171–2, 222–3
winning, organising to win
  15–17

Wood, John 102
working hours 196

**Y**
Ye Olde Oak 76–7
*Yes: 50 Secrets from the Science
  of Persuasion* (Goldstein,
  Martin and Cialdini, 2007)
  93–4